MORE KICKS THAN PENCE

.RD

A NOTE ON THE AUTHOR

Michael O'Toole was born in Hospital, County Limerick in 1938. He was educated there by the Presentation sisters and the De La Salle brothers and later at the Polytechnic of Central London and Trinity College, Dublin. He lives with his family in Portmarnock, Co Dublin.

MORE KICKS THAN PENCE

A LIFE IN IRISH JOURNALISM

Michael O'Toole

POOLBEG

First published 1992 by
Poolbeg Press Ltd
Knocksedan House,
Swords, Co Dublin, Ireland

© Michael O'Toole, 1992

The moral right of the author has been asserted.

ISBN 1 85371 143 8

A catalogue record for this book is available from the British Library.

Cover design by Pomphrey Associates
Set by Richard Parfrey in ITC Stone Serif 9.5/15
Printed by The Guernsey Press Company Ltd,
Vale, Guernsey, Channel Islands

FOR MAUREEN

ACKNOWLEDGEMENTS

With a work of this kind, one's first debt is to the colleagues, living and dead, who appear in the text, and I gratefully acknowledge that debt here. I should also like to thank a large number of people who helped me in the writing of this book, in particular Margaret Daly (without whose encouragement it wouldn't have been written at all), Miss Betty, Arthur Flynn, David Davin-Power, Nora Lucey, Frank Corr, Adrian MacLoughlin, Hector Legge, and, of course, my editor, Sean McMahon.

Hugh Leonard, Maeve Binchy and Brendan Kennelly kindly read the manuscript and comented on it. Tommy McCann and Jim Griffiths of the *Irish Press* library were unfailingly helpful to me, as were the staff of the National Library of Ireland. I owe a particular debt of gratitude to Ann Gallagher, daughter of the founding editor, Frank Gallagher, for permission to quote from her father's papers in the National Library. Irish Press Newspapers and the editor-in-chief, Dr Eamon de Valera, were especially generous in allowing the use of copyright photographs. I am grateful to Douglas E Duggan for the picture of his friend and colleague, the late Maurice Liston.

As always there was the support and encouragement of my wife, Maureen, who, along with my mother and my children, Orla, Feargal and Justin, helped in thousands of ways.

CONTENTS

FOREWORD

Those who run the journalism colleges should think of Nicholas Tomalin and forget about the points system. Tomalin, a distinguished correspondent of *The Sunday Times* when *The Sunday Times* was a distinguished newspaper, declared that the only qualities essential for success in journalism were "ratlike cunning, a plausible manner and a little literary ability." Another advantage, he said, was the ability to steal other people's ideas and phrases. And to drive home his point, he added that the "ratlike cunning" bit of his first sentence had been invented by his colleague Murray Sayle. Malcolm Muggeridge, another sage of the journalism trade, saw it in different terms. "Journalists," he wrote, "follow authority as sharks follow a liner, dining on the scraps that are thrown overboard."

Cheats, scavengers, sycophants and cute hoors and, strangely, the odd saint too, not to mention the bohemians and the eccentrics. It takes all sorts to make a newsroom.

When I drifted into journalism at the ripe old age of twenty-three the bohemians and the eccentrics were still thick on the ground. There was a man who rode a bicycle to which he had attached a large sail. Another, when drunk, made a habit of prostrating himself like a mediaeval monk before the night news editor chanting and begging pardon "for all misdemeanours, past, present and to come."

Even though Flann O'Brien was taking satiric licence when he wrote that any piece of *Irish Press* copy which didn't bear the imprint of the bottom of a porter bottle from Mulligan's or the White Horse would automatically be held suspect and spiked by the chief sub, there was a fearsome amount of hard drinking. The 1973 productivity agreement which changed many things in Burgh Quay stated blandly there would be "full co-operation in the observance of proper standards of conduct and in this regard it is recognised that there is a certain problem concerning drink."

The bohemians and the eccentrics have largely gone now, their places taken by bright college kids who have written brilliant essays with titles like "The Quantitative Assessment of the Theory of Sexual Offensiveness and Feminism in the New Communications Revolution," and "Revolutionary Angst in the Communications Theory of Klement Gottwald."

When I went into journalism I was naïve, unlettered and, worst of all, under the crass misapprehension that journalists were universally loved. I believed that the Irish looked upon the journalist as some kind of lay *sagart aroon*— a man who may on occasion have to utter a harsh word or draw attention to unpleasant truths but who is, nevertheless, loved and admired for having to so do. I believed that the *Daily Mail* and the *Daily Express* were great newspapers; that Northcliffe was already a saint and Beaverbrook well on the way to becoming one. I was fired with impossibly romantic notions about the old black art.

And I was determined to save Ireland.

It didn't take long to discover that among the ranks of us journalists there was only a handful who gave any thought to saving Ireland.

Many were born sycophants ever ready to bend the news—or their views of it—to suit the whim of proprietor, prelate or politician. Others were natural propagandists with an unhealthy desire to dominate the minds of the readers and decide for them what they should read and how they should think. There were the indolent ones who would spin any line that was thrown to them provided it saved them from having to think or to make another phone call. And there were the sybarites who used their press cards as meal tickets and had long abandoned all pretence of independence and impartiality.

There were a few men and women of real integrity who were serious about their craft and willing to endure contumely or even physical danger in order to practise it. These were the kind of people WH Auden had in mind when he wrote: "With all that can be said, justly, against journalists, there is one kind of journalist to whom civilisation owes a very real debt, namely, the brave and honest reporter who unearths and makes public unpleasant facts, cases of injustice, cruelty, corruption, which the authorities would like to keep hidden, and which the average reader would prefer not to be compelled to think about."

But the majority, like the majority in any other profession, were decent people who performed their mundane tasks reasonably well and went to considerable lengths to avoid trouble. Had any of them encountered the burning bush their first thought would be to send for the fire brigade.

Looking back across the divide of three decades what strikes me most about those early years in journalism is the marvellous, almost incessant sense of fun. Like the young rustic in Thomas Hardy's poem:

> I did not know
> That heydays fade and go,
> But deemed that what was would always be so.

Then, when I was about ten years in journalism, an insignificant thing happened which had a profound effect on me. While I was on a boring assignment in one of the boring Scandinavian capitals, a young civil servant from Iveagh House who hadn't mastered the most fundamental of all the diplomatic skills—the ability to hold one's liquor—said to me at the dinner table: "You appear to be a reasonably decent sort of person. Doesn't it worry you that you belong to such a rapacious profession?"

The observation at least had the virtue of directness. For me it was the first clear signal of the build-up of resentment of the media in Ireland which would soon become almost a torrent. The age of innocence was over.

In his valedictory piece in *Time* a couple of years ago the distinguished media critic Thomas Griffith asked a question which had been troubling him for years. "Why is it," he wrote, "that journalism is so much better than it was, yet the public is more troubled by its performance than it used to be?"

It is a question that has puzzled me too. There is hardly anything about which I am certain, but I passionately believe that Irish journalism is in an infinitely better state of health today than it was when I started learning the trade three decades ago. Today's journalists are more professional, more confident and better educated than we were. And Irish society is far more open now than it was then. Why is it then that scarcely a week passes without some bishop, government minister or other potentate leaping into the headlines bemoaning the sins of the media and the woeful decline in journalistic standards.

The answer probably lies in the Egyptian proverb which warns those whose business it is to reveal the truth of things that it is as well to keep one foot in the stirrup at all times.

The media revolution that started in the Sixties has changed the world. It is only natural that the power brokers who came to maturity in an age when journalists could easily be fobbed off with a press release and a few blandishments would whinge, whine and howl at changes which threaten their power and authority. Alas, the concept of the reporter as representative citizen has never caught on in Ireland and, if the attitude surveys are correct, the Irish don't think highly of their journalists. That is a pity but it is understandable.

This book is not an attempt at a history of Irish journalism during the thirty or so years that I have been part of it, nor is it a history of the *Irish Press*. It is simply a memoir of my own very often mundane role. There are no sensational revelations, no scandals, no great pronouncements. I have not set out to make propaganda either for the trade of journalism or for the newspaper group where I have happily spent most of my working life. In both cases I am as aware of their faults as their virtues and I have tried to be as fair and as objective as it is possible for me to be. I was particularly fortunate in that I went into journalism just before its transition from a very ramshackle, disorganised and often quite crazy industry to a cut-throat, very serious and rather sanitised business. I have tried to capture something of those earlier carefree and more innocent days in the *Evening Press* newsroom when the paper—the outstanding publishing success of its time—was pushing ahead of its rivals and life seemed "a quite unlosable game."

I have written about my years as the Dubliner's Diary columnist of the *Evening Press* and of the originator of that column, the imperious, suave and—to his friends— immensely kindhearted Terry O'Sullivan. I have said something about my time on local newspapers and touched on some themes that have interested me, especially aviation, church-media relations and the relationship of journalism and commerce.

But my main concern has been with people. In "The Municipal Gallery Revisited," Yeats asked that he be judged "not by this book or that" but that his glory should lie in the marvellous friendships he had enjoyed. Working in Burgh Quay has always been akin to living directly over the San Andreas fault: shocks and tremors are frequent, and the prospect of the ultimate catastrophe is always at the back of the mind. Like the good folk who live along the San Andreas, one gets used to the shocks and tremors. Even at the worst of times in Burgh Quay there was always great camaraderie and wonderful friendships. That this should be so is often a mystery to outsiders but those of us who inhabit the quake zone know the answer.

Looking round for a title for this book I thought of standing that Sixties song on its head and calling it "Even the Good Times were Bad." But that would be a bit unfair... And so, in keeping with that journalistic tradition of which Nicholas Tomalin wrote, I filched my title—from Patrick Kavanagh...

> More kicks than pence
> We get from commonsense...

1

ONE OF DEV'S MEN

The *Irish Press* was created by me out of the most mixed
elements, trained, partly trained and untrained...

Frank Gallagher, founding editor

My arrival in Burgh Quay coincided with one of Major
Vivion de Valera's periodic economy drives. This may have
had a bearing on why I was hired in the first place, for
even though I was twenty-six I had been a late entrant to
journalism and was in no position to look for more than
the minimum wage. And at this time the *Irish Press* was
losing some of the best journalists in the country because
of a reluctance to make up the paltry extra sums—often as
little as five shillings a week—that these people could earn
elsewhere.

On that crisp early autumn morning in 1964 the lady
in the front office of what was once the Tivoli music hall
looked me up and down like a drill-sergeant before signalling
to an insolent-looking youth sitting on a stack of newspapers
and sucking a Woodbine. "Take this gentleman up to the
newsroom to Mr Redmond," she instructed with the

resigned air of a midwife who has been roused prematurely by a foolish young husband.

We passed through a creaky door which slammed back violently only to be checked at the last moment by a thick leather strap. "Are you another reporter then?" inquired the insolent one as he plodded unwillingly up the stairs. I admitted that this was the case. The boy stopped and looked back at me, a twisted grin on his face. "O Jaysus," he said very slowly and led me into the big room where I was to spend most of my working life.

From the newsroom door I beheld a large serge-sheathed posterior arched over the biggest wastepaper basket I had ever seen. All the detritus of the newsroom—old newspapers, press releases, tealeaves, twisted balls of copy paper—flew through the air as a result of its furious excavation. I assumed that some item of great importance—tomorrow's leading article perhaps—had been mislaid and was now being sought in this mountain of rubbish. Flushed and half breathless, the bulky figure at last straightened itself, clutching the objects of all the endeavour, a dozen or so used envelopes with gum intact which could be used for the house post. The Major's economy drives, like those of that other remarkable newspaper publisher, Lord Beaverbrook, went deep and were taken seriously by his managing editor.

William J Redmond—WJR to his contemporaries, Big Daddy to irreverent newsroom fledgelings—wore sombre serge suits and used his black horn-rimmed glasses to great intimidatory effect. Feared, flattered and fêted, he had been the undisputed master of the newsroom for almost a quarter of a century. He was gruff to the point of rudeness and unwilling to listen to any point of view save the official one, and it is easy to see how his reputation for tyranny took root. It was unjustified—WJR was himself the victim of a system which in the words of the paper's first literary editor, MJ MacManus, had created "an atmosphere of desolation, gloom, suspicion and intrigue." He lived in constant fear of the major and like all the early executives of the *Irish Press*, he had to deal with a rag-bag staff that was made up of a sprinkling of talented professionals and numerous untrained and sometimes quite unbalanced eccentrics, former gunmen, republican faithful and downright rogues.

Only thirty-three years had elapsed between the foundation of the paper and my arrival—and thirty-three years in the history of a national newspaper is but the tick of a clock. That morning I was woefully ignorant of that or indeed any history. I did not then appreciate how recent were the euphoric days when the great founder stalked the building, supervising everyone, criticising the leaders, delegating nothing. More importantly, I did not then understand how close we were to many of the powerful myths which the founder's "great enterprise" (as he liked to call it) has helped to generate. I did not know then that many of our boasts were hollow and were leading us into a territory hostile and dangerous enough to threaten our very existence.

Like many youngsters of peasant origin, I had grown up with the *Irish Press*. My grandfather, Michael O'Toole, revered Eamon de Valera. He saw him as the leader who would liberate the poor man from his hovel and his ignorance and create some Celtic Shangri-La where dwelt the comely maidens and their camán-wielding swains. If my grandfather was sitting by his wireless on St Patrick's Day, 1943, listening to his hero inviting him to share his dream of "a land whose countryside would be bright with...the laughter of comely maidens," I have no doubt but that he had tears in his eyes.

While I would have known the paper since I started to read Captain Mac's column at the age of four or thereabouts, my first clear memory of its bold news-laden front page dates from Saturday, 11 January, 1952. That was the day after the crash of the Aer Lingus DC-3 *St Kevin* in Snowdonia, and I can still vividly remember walking out of Mitchell's shop in Hospital with that direful front page in my hands. In those pre-TV days the impact of a dramatic black-and-white photograph and well-presented news story was infinitely greater than now when our minds have become jaded and numbed from the constant bombardment of images and words.

A few images of that first morning in Burgh Quay remain vivid: I was struck by the dinginess of the big room with its long custom-made reporter's table, the telephone wires dropping from the ceiling, the horseshoe-shaped table where the sub-editors sat. The deadline for the first edition of the *Evening Press* was approaching and there was a *frisson* in the air that I hadn't experienced elsewhere. Tony Gallagher, a tough ex-Fleet Street man and the senior reporter on the *Evening Press* cadre, was working on the lead story and in a voice that might be heard on O'Connell Bridge he was trying to extract details from some lethargic country correspondent. Now he was upbraiding this unwilling correspondent, demanding, "What the hell does it matter if the parish priest won't like it?" and "You had better make up your mind as to whether you want to be a press correspondent or the parish priest's self-appointed censor."

While I now found myself working in the newsroom pool—meaning that I could be assigned on an hourly basis to any of the three papers—my objective from the start was to get on the small permanent staff of the evening paper. As far as newspapers are concerned, the *Evening Press* was my first great love and much of my freelance work had been directed towards it. Here I had what for the time was a reasonable evening newspaper scoop by breaking the story of the engagement of Brendan Bowyer, then one of the biggest names in Irish show business. Brendan had confirmed the engagement to me in his dressing room in Lawlor's Ballroom, Naas but when it appeared in print there was a denial as his handlers felt it would diminish his popularity. Every reporter knows the frustration of having a story denied because its telling doesn't suit the requirements of the moment. This particular denial had the potential to do a great deal of damage to an unknown and inexperienced reporter. The *Evening Press* printed the denial in the late-news column of the first edition while my story stood on the front page. Fortunately for me, the news editor, Sean Ward, believed my version and in due course when Brendan and Stella were married I was vindicated. Brendan and I have often had a laugh over the incident since but at the time I was very upset indeed.

In the true traditions of Burgh Quay, I had barely sat down that first morning when I was given a job. Sean Ward called me up to the newsdesk, handed me a small bundle of newspaper cuttings from the library and said: "Give me six or seven paragraphs of an obituary on this fellow, and remember the first edition deadline is ten thirty."

It was the simplest of assignments—no more than fifteen minutes work for any reasonably competent reporter. And six or seven paragraphs—on the *Limerick Leader* we'd be thinking in terms of at least a column.

But now panic began to set in. Did the *Press* have a particular style for obits? (It did—a very plain and straightforward one. The reporter who started off an obit of a veteran of the war of independence with the line, "The old gunman is dead," was severely reprimanded.) Would I get the intro right? Would I miss out on some vital detail of the man's career? Would the chief sub, guardian against all solecism and inaccuracy, send my piece back with some glaring horror ringed in blue pencil?

I shouldn't have worried. I have no way of knowing what our chief sub, Terry Doorley, thought of my first modest contribution as a staff reporter as it passed over his desk that morning. When the first edition came up an hour and a half later I was relieved to find my piece nicely displayed in column eight of page one—and exactly as I had written it.

Terry Doorley was a tall, lumbering man with thick spectacles and an acerbic tongue who was nicknamed "Clumper" after the rabbit in J. Ashton Freeman's "Wild Wisdom" feature. Every time a new reporter arrived Terry would ask the news editor where the new arrival had come from, and if it was outside the Pale he would intone: "Another bloody illiterate who thinks there are two 'k's in Shankill." He had worked in South Africa and had little sympathy for blacks. Scratching around for a lead for the first edition one morning he asked Adrian MacLoughlin of the foreign desk if anything interesting was ticking over from the agencies. Adrian said there had just been a UPI flash about a pit collapse in South Africa which had killed thirty miners. "Are they black miners or white miners?" the chief sub demanded. Adrian said he presumed they were black miners. "In that case," said Terry, "we'll give them a strong single on page three."

I had scarcely finished my obituary notice that morning when behind me a great and strange voice boomed out: "They tell me we have a decent man from Limerick here at last." Turning, I found myself looking at a giant of a man with a face like an enormous turnip out of which shone two mischievous blue eyes. The huge frame was covered with a Denis Guiney gaberdine coat and on its head was a grey felt hat which had been sat on in many a snug. "I'm Liston from Knockaderry," the strange voice said as I got a playful thump between the shoulder blades.

I had, of course, heard of Maurice Liston, doyen of the agricultural correspondents and founding member of the NUJ in Ireland, who was at that time one of the outstanding figures of Irish journalism. He didn't normally frequent the newsroom at that time, he told me, but he had come this morning as a fellow Limerick man to mark my cards. It was true, he said, that Burgh Quay was a cruel and a dangerous place but one shouldn't believe everything one heard about it. "Expect a good kick in the balls every two hours or so and you won't be too far out," Maurice advised. "And always be nice to the copy boy, because as sure as Jesus he'll be the news editor next year."

The grin turned into a belly-laugh and the great frame heaved with mirth. Then pointing to a serene old lady who appeared to be dozing or lost in reverie at the other end of the long table, Maurice said in a conspiratorial whisper, "That's Máire Comerford. Whatever else you do, never cross her. She shot a Black and Tan in 1921 and she still has the revolver tucked up the leg of her bloomers."

Máire Comerford's career as a journalist had all but ended when I came to Burgh Quay. Like WJR she came from Wexford. But she was reputed to be of a higher caste and this, coupled with her impeccable Republican credentials and the fact that she had a direct line to the man in the Park, put WJR and nearly everyone else in awe of her. She was an indifferent reporter but her fearlessness was legendary. Maureen Craddock, WJR's secretary, who was a confidante of hers used to tell of Máire 's experience when she fell into the hands of the Black and Tans. As a softening-up process in her interrogation, she was locked in a room with a corpse and the lamp removed. When her captors opened the door the following morning they found the corpse on the floor and Máire sleeping peacefully in the bed.

At this time Maurice was well established as one of the legends of Irish journalism. When he joined the *Irish Press* in 1932 he was a highly trained reporter who, like myself, had cut his teeth on the *Limerick Leader*. He had also served the cause in the West Limerick brigade of the IRA and after escaping from the Curragh was never recaptured. He took no pension and rarely talked about his exploits. The only time I ever heard him discuss them was when he came into the Scotch House one evening after having a chest X-ray and he told me that the specialist on looking at the film said: "I see that you had pneumonia, Mr Liston." Maurice insisted that he had never been treated for pneumonia but as he was leaving the hospital he suddenly remembered a hideous week of coughing and fever as he slept in ditches while he was on the run. For his services to the NUJ he had received the union's highest and rarest accolade, being made a "member of honour."

One of the many remarkable things about Maurice Liston was his voice. No one I ever met before or since spoke even remotely like him. It was as if the words were being sucked up from his throat and filtered through coarse gravel as they came out. His was truly a language that the stranger did not know. Once, at an annual delegate meeting of the NUJ in Brighton, the English delegates called for a speech from the father-figure of the union in Ireland. Maurice had been in search of what he liked to describe as "formidable drink" and he rose somewhat unsteadily to respond. As the applause faded he began to speak. "For five years of my life," he began, "I fought the fucking British." Then he sat down. The delegates, understanding not a word he had said and believing that he was overcome with emotion, gave him a standing ovation.

It wasn't only the voice that contributed to his unique

delivery. Though by no means taciturn he was economical with words and often arranged them oddly. One anecdote about him which I have heard recounted by newspaper people in many parts of the world concerns a fire in a Dublin convent during the 1940s. WJR was then at the height of his powers as a disciplinarian and as they were both departing to their separate pubs for a nightcap he ordered Maurice to get a taxi and follow the brigade. Half an hour later WJR left the Scotch House for Mulligan's where he found Maurice propped up at the counter with "a formidable drink." "Mr Liston," he demanded (WJR was always formal in confrontation), "what about the fire in the Dominican convent?" Maurice was unruffled. "I was speaking to the reverend mother," he said, "and she told me personally that there was fuck all in it."

Yet despite this and other displays of bravado, Maurice, like most of the reporters of his generation, was essentially a timid man. They had reason to be. From the foundation of the state until well into the 1960s Irish journalism suffered from the general paralysis that afflicted Irish society. There was an almost complete failure on the part of newspapers to apply decent critical analysis to practically any aspect of Irish life. In *Ireland: A Social and Cultural History 1922-1985*, Terence Brown says:

Regrettably, almost all Irish journalism in the period had contented itself with the reportage of events and the propagandist reiteration of the familiar terms of Irish political and cultural debate until these categories became mere counters and slogans often remote from actualities.

The reporting, more often than not, was on the terms and under the control of the authority figures—which is the real reason why ageing politicians, prelates and sundry potentates pine for the days of the old-style journalism. The journalists in the main were poorly educated, poorly motivated and poorly paid. They went about their work in the sure knowledge that in the event of any complaint from the great and powerful they would almost certainly get no backing. In the early 1960s an *Irish Press* photographer with a wife and family was suspended from duty for a week because in a caption he inadvertently portrayed a senior army officer as being one rank lower than he was.

Maurice and many of his contemporaries were journalists of a kind which, though still common in the Sixties, is now virtually extinct. Bohemian by temperament, they had drifted into a little world which though frequently called a profession imposed no qualifications for entry and enforced no real standards for remaining. In Maurice's case he had run away from a farm and endured the splendid irony of being made into an agricultural correspondent. Many of his peers had tried other vocations and either found them wanting or had themselves been found wanting. A number had been in the religious life. Some could be classified among the incorrigibly eccentric—if not the mentally unbalanced. Many were improvident and impecunious and lived in dread of their bank managers.

Many failed to understand that being called to the banquet is not the same as being part of the feast and foolishly forgot that a journalist is always an outsider looking in. They knew that by observing a few ground rules they could just about survive and preserve their sense of their own courage as well. Above all, they observed the rules of that special Geneva convention of Irish public life which declares: thou shall not queer the pitch. Like Mark Twain, they would have liked nothing better than to blow the gaff on the whole world—except that they were acutely aware of the perils of so doing. They were not so much paper tigers as tissue-paper tigers.

I am not trying to deprecate them. Like all of us, they were children of their own times and it was not their fault that they lived in an age of brutal stagnancy. Nor do I wish to convey that the slicker, better-educated, better-accoutred journalists who followed them are invariably superior. Very often the opposite is true. The call to the rich man's table is as attractive and as fatal as ever and the line between fact and propaganda is often blurred now as it was then. Despite all the advantages by way of education, decent salaries, training and trade-union protection there is still too much mediocre journalism in Ireland. A large number of Irish journalists still fail to make the fundamental distinction between the "news" that is handed to them along with a gin and tonic by some PR person and that which has to be painfully and skilfully prised from a hostile and unwilling source. Northcliffe's dictum that "news is what someone somewhere wishes to suppress" and that "everything else is advertising" seems to have little effect on a large number of Irish journalists.

By the 1960s the insular world in which Irish journalists worked was at last beginning to change. The close of the previous decade had seen a Vatican council convened and Aer Lingus spreading its wings across the north Atlantic. Now there were Irish soldiers working (and being killed) with the UN in Africa. These were milestones in the progress of Irish life and journalists went out to report on them. Prior to this, foreign coverage seemed to be more or less restricted to the annual Dublin diocesan pilgrimage to Lourdes and, in the case of the *Irish Press*, to the odd foreign trip made by Mr de Valera.

There was, however, plenty of movement within the country. Maurice Liston and his contemporaries travelled far and wide—first class, on free passes provided by the railway companies—far more than reporters do today. The assignments were usually mundane—agricultural shows, amateur drama festivals, the consecration of some bishop— the stuff of which Irish national newspapers of the day were chiefly fashioned.

These excursions were admirably suited to the bohemian temperament. They entitled the traveller to viaticum in the form of advance expenses, often grudgingly handed over, which wouldn't have to be paid back for weeks and which were sometimes severely dented in Mulligan's prior to departure. They ensured a temporary respite from the tyranny of the newsdesk and provided the opportunity of looking up old friends and acquaintances. For like all commercial travellers, these men had an extensive network of cronies and like-minded souls to be found in all sorts of nooks and corners throughout the country.

Joe Shakespeare—one of the early *Irish Press* photographers, who claimed that he named his son William to ensure that no one would ever give him a job as a reporter—routed all his journeys via Kilcullen so as to call on Joe McTernan in his pub. Donal Foley, who got his start in the *Irish Press* and went on to play a major role in the development of *The Irish Times,* once set off to cover a Munster final in Thurles instructing his driver to "put the boot down now and don't stop till you get to Ryan's of Parkgate Street."

Kevin Collins was another of these worthies. He moved constantly from job to job, drawing his paltry superannuation entitlement each time and spending it before moving on to the next house. These moves were taken for granted, although on his final return to *The Irish Times* a testy old sub-editor after welcoming him back added, "And I sincerely hope you're staying this time, Kevin, because I'm damned if I'll subscribe to another gold watch for you." Kevin sailed through life with a smile and an aura of dignified tranquillity which, though aided by alcohol, was a true expression of his gentle soul. Well over six feet tall, erect even in his cups as a guardsman at the Trooping the Colour and with a head of which an emperor, Roman or otherwise, would feel proud, he loved all luxuries like the true sybarite he was and he had a great talent for getting himself invited to lunch.

He was recently arrived in Burgh Quay when I came up from Limerick and in my naïveté I got the impression that he was some sort of social editor in charge of reporting luncheons and dinners. Most afternoons at around three Kevin would glide into the newsroom, the little veins that criss-crossed his nose and cheeks nicely suffused by wine, and having taken his place at the big table, would proceed to open the top button of his trousers. There would follow, for anyone who cared to listen, a dissertation on that day's culinary delights. Dining out, even for journalists, was then relatively rare and these commentaries were received with a mixture of awe and envy by a hard-nosed crew, most of whom wouldn't have been able to afford a bacon and egg in the Savoy on the way home.

"I must say the young chef in the Royal Hibernian is coming on by leaps and bounds," Kevin, even more flushed than usual, announced one afternoon before resting his head on his unopened typewriter in anticipation of a little doze. Although he wrote well, Kevin was not in love with work and it took a great amount of effort by the news editors to get him started.

On this occasion he was being pestered by a junior reporter who had been covering the same function for the evening paper and who, though barely able to stand, was insisting that something should be written if only to show appreciation for the fabulous meal. Kevin would have none of it but the youngster continued with his drunken urgings. Shaken out of his reverie he eventually drew himself up to his full height and thundered: "Write absolutely nothing, young man. Let us astonish them with our ingratitude."

As well as luncheons Kevin attended a large number of cocktail parties. While he was on the *Irish Press* the kind of 6pm reception which was to become a commonplace of journalistic life in Dublin was evolving. Cynical in their conception and often mindlessly boring in their execution, these affairs usually took place in hotel rooms with squeaky floors. They were frequented on the one hand by freeloading journalists who had as much interest in the real reason for the party as a hermit might have in a weekend at Butlin's and on the other by beady-eyed young PR executives who would have convinced themselves that the product, be it a new wire scrubber or a vile new brand of plonk, was the greatest gift to humanity since penicillin.

Kevin had devised a series of protocols to insulate him against the punishments of these affairs. Positioning himself within an easy leap of the exit, he would—provided there was somewhere else to go—vanish Houdini-like in the split second between the opening of the speaker's mouth and the utterance of the first syllable of his speech. He also perfected a system of nonspeak for these occasions which repulsed all but the most brazen bores. This consisted of muttering strings of meaningless and disjointed short phrases punctuated with numerous "uh-uh"s, "ahem"s and "eh-eh"s delivered in an undertone so perfectly pitched that the astounded listener would crane over in a desperate effort to comprehend the incomprehensible. Kevin would then repeat the gibberish, smiling amiably all the time, until the confused and embarrassed recipient excused himself and fled, leaving Kevin in peace to enjoy his whiskey.

It was typical of Kevin that in death, as in life, he would arrange the best for himself. He faced his last illness with exemplary courage and during the course of it he went down to St Patrick's Cathedral and interviewed the dean about his obsequies. Kevin had earlier embraced the *via media* and he had a special affection for St Patrick's with its Swiftian connection, its great musical tradition and its Anglican liturgy based on the majestic English of the King James Bible and the 1926 revision of the Book of Common Prayer. These things were important to him. After the funeral of a colleague Kevin came up to me in the Silver Swan and remarked how he would hate to go out "with some parish priest mouthing clichés over me amid the plaster statues."

Along with practically every journalist in Dublin I went along to St Patrick's to bid Kevin farewell. As the coffin was brought in and placed in the choir beneath the banners of the knights of St Patrick, I reflected that Kevin, installed in whatever section of paradise is reserved for sybaritic and fun-loving Irish journalists, must be well satisfied with the turn-out.

At the bottom of the nave—the longest nave in Ireland— the funeral procession that Kevin had organised for himself was assembling. Led by the processional cross, the choir would soon pass through the cathedral beside the spot where Swift, the greatest journalist Ireland ever produced, lies beside his beloved Stella. It would pass the place where is displayed Swift's epitaph with its awesome injunction which makes the heart of every true journalist quicken:

Go traveller, and imitate if you can, his strenuous vindication of men's liberty.

From the end of the nave the dean invokes the names of the Trinity; the great Willis organ sounds and the choir takes up Henry Lyte's mournful prayer of supplication:

Abide with me: fast falls the eventide;
The darkness deepens; Lord, with me abide:
When other helpers fail, and comforts flee,
Help of the helpless, O abide with me.

We Irish have little talent for the procession as an art
form—that is one skill that we did not inherit from our
imperial masters. There are, I believe, only two places in
Ireland where the art of the procession is tolerably executed:
Trinity College and St Patrick's Cathedral. At St Patrick's
when the all-male procession moves through the nave (it
was a paradox of the St Patrick's of the time that the liberal
theology of the place co-existed most comfortably with a
liturgical conservatism which not only scorned the new
prayer book but steadfastly refused to allow women in the
choir) it seems to be saying: "Look at us. Here we are.
We've been doing this for eight hundred years. We are
extremely good at it. This is our place. Here is where we
belong."

The choristers in their cassocks of St Patrick's blue,
hymnals held breast high, are followed by the cathedral
clergy. The dean's vicar, Canon Cecil Bradley, half-moon
glasses perched on the end of his nose, glides over the tiled
floor. The dean and ordinary, the Very Rev Dr Victor Griffin,
seventy-sixth successor of Jonathan Swift, is slightly bowed,
his medal of office hanging on a ribbon of that same blue
and the crest of St Patrick's embossed on his black stole.

> Swift to its close ebbs out life's little day;
>
> Earth's joys grow dim, its glories pass away;
>
> Change and decay in all around I see:
>
> O Thou who changest not, abide with me.

We all loved Kevin and we would miss him greatly. But outside his family circle this was not an occasion of real grief. Considering his lifestyle, Kevin had had a good run. Pan, his wife, was a woman of strong faith and she had a good job as chief researcher to *The Late Late Show*. The children were mature young adults. So when something very funny happened during the service none of us felt guilty at enjoying it.

As is common on these occasions, one of the priests speaks or chants certain praises regarding the deceased. Canon Bradley's fine clerical voice now thrilled up to the rafters as he intoned: "Let us give thanks to God for the life of Kevin and for his great services to journalism."

In the hush of the great cathedral I thought I felt the stirring of an incipient guffaw. Beside me Cathal O'Shannon, an old friend of Kevin's, buried his head in his hands in an effort to stifle his mirth.

I can see clearly now that the canon and the order of service were quite correct. Kevin did make a big contribution to Irish journalism, not in the conventional sense of covering big stories, winning awards or exposing great scandals, but through his comradeship, his sense of fun and the sheer exuberance of his personality.

Looking back through "the weariness, the fever and the

fret" that the passing years bring to all of us, I marvel at how carefree, how uncomplicated and how crazy those early years in Burgh Quay really were. Of course there were serious people about but from this remove it seems that to a man and to a woman the companions of my youth were all intent on calling the bluff on the whole world—and would have done, had they been given half the chance.

They flit in and out of my memory like figures in an old newsreel: Sean Lynch flashing his cuffs in the Silver Swan as he told us about sorties he had flown in the Vietnam he had never seen; Des Twomey rising up indignant in the subs room casting the copy of some long-winded reporter into a wastepaper basket and declaring: "Better I should go for a libation than preside over the desecration of the language of Shakespeare and Milton..."; Adrian MacLoughlin arriving at the foreign desk on the day Vincent Jennings took over as editor of the *Sunday Press* singing, "The working class can kiss my arse/I've got the foreman's job at last"; Terry O'Sullivan confronted in his office by a feminist who pulled up her sweater to reveal her breasts; a sub-editor, very drunk and stripped to the waist, struggling to throw the chief sub's large wooden chair over the quay wall and into the Liffey...

In the Sixties such conduct was tolerated to a degree that astonished people in saner workplaces. And for those of us who were young in the Sixties life seemed to be one long, hilarious party. Two of our three papers were top of the league. We chased hard after the news stories and we knew that we were part of what was regarded as the finest news-gathering machine in the country. We spent most of

our money in the Silver Swan and gave not a thought to
the morrow.

2

A FOOT IN THE DOOR

Suppose they are not rewarded with much money or dignity or fame; suppose they are debarred from having the life of a normal man; suppose they wield no power while they last, and cannot last long? What of it? They each yell more, sweat more, hiss more, start more tears and gooseflesh in the course of their lives than a dozen ordinary men. They have a helluva good time.

Gerald W Thompson, *Baltimore Sun*

The first newsroom I ever set foot in was that of the *Limerick Weekly Echo and District Advertiser*. Newsroom is perhaps too grandiose a term for that section of what was essentially a large lean-to clinging to the gaunt limestone frontage of the former Presbyterian church that houses McKern's Printing works. The chief—and only—reporter was a man called Christy Bannon who drank large quantities of black rum washed down with bottles of stout. Christy had been a barber and he had drifted into journalism through bringing in snippets of news that he picked up in his shop. He wore a soft brown hat, *Front Page* style, and an expression of intense woe. Pat Finn, the photographer, said that in a previous incarnation Christy must have been covering the Agony in the Garden and that the face stuck. Christy spoke sparingly and cynically. He was one of those people who had known practically everyone he knew before any of them had an arse to their trousers.

TP (Tommy) Morris, the editor, was the brother of the *Echo*'s proprietor, Ivan Morris, who had a printing business in Dublin, and they had known Christy when they were youngsters and they all played soccer together. Tommy frequently complained about his protégé. "There was a time when Christy would do the 'wall of death' for a story," the editor would say, shaking his head in resignation and pointing through the window to the slight and apathetic figure huddled over the two-bar electric fire in the corner of the lean-to.

According to Tommy, Christy's transition from barbering to news-gathering came one busy afternoon when Christy, who had been drinking tea in the office, was asked if he would mind running down to Cruise's to pick up a press release from the Irish Creamery Milk Suppliers Association. "The next thing was I had a delegation from the NUJ complaining that their member wasn't getting a living wage," Tommy said.

Although lively and voluble when on a licensed premises (Christy would never call it a pub) in the office he had the true detachment of the mystic. Threats and entreaties wafted over him with as much effect as the smoke from his eternal Gold Flake. It was claimed that he had been fired six times but on each occasion turned up for work in the lean-to on the following Monday, explaining to the embarrassed clerk in the front office that "Tommy was only joking."

The story went that when he turned up for work on the Monday after being sacked for the sixth time, Tommy called him into his office on the other side of the lean-to and had a serious talk with him. "How many times have you been sacked, Christy?" the editor asked.

"Several times, Tommy," said Christy.

"And were you given notice on all these occasions?" asked Tommy.

"Indeed I was," Christy said.

"And on this last occasion were you given notice by the firm's solicitors?"

"I was, Tommy."

"Were your cards sent to you by registered post?"

"They were, Tommy."

"And was everything explained to you?"

"Yes," replied Christy, showing signs of boredom.

There was a pause, broken eventually by Morris. "What have you to say to all this, Christy?" he asked solemnly.

"All I have to say, Tommy," said Christy rather tartly, "is that this ball-hopping will have to stop."

I learned a great deal about journalism in the lean-to. Like Christy, I was a blow-in, an interloper in this crazy world of journalism who hoped that if I hung around long enough I too might be called upon to do the "wall of death" for a story.

At this time I was working as a kitchen clerk in Shannon Airport. A digest article about Caesar Ritz had turned me into the Dick Whittington of the hotel industry—one day

I would go to London, not to be anything silly like lord mayor, but to manage the Savoy. There was no question of being able to afford going to hotel school, so I started to work my way through the various departments. I did eventually go to London—not to manage the Savoy but to do my City and Guilds and study for associate membership of the Hotel and Catering Institute. I worked as a waiter, a barman, a kitchen porter, a cook, a cellar man...

I was soon disillusioned. The digest article had been strong on the glamour of the hotel industry but woefully weak on what went on in the kitchens, the cellars, the staff halls, the offices. I must have disliked the catering industry from the start but I can remember quite clearly when I first became conscious of actually hating it. This epiphany, Joycean in its intensity, occurred when a stately head waiter glided through the kitchen doors, stopped suddenly in his tracks like a ballerina after a leap and let off a thunderous fart as he applied his gold cigarette lighter to a Churchman No 1. It wasn't so much that I minded the physical act of his farting—there were worse crudities in hotel kitchens in those days—but this particular fart, radiating through the kitchen like a signal from a radio transmitter, became for me a symbol of all the sham, all the sycophancy, all the fawning and insincerity that the hotel industry uses for oxygen. The notion of being manager of the Savoy had suddenly become repugnant.

More and more I found myself drawn to the lean-to beside the Dominican Church in Baker Place. Across the road was the Lyric Cinema, where on a beautiful summer's evening a few years earlier I had queued with my first love, a local beauty named Peggy Guerrini, to see the current sensation, *Rock Around the Clock*. As the shadows lengthened that evening there came wafting from the church across the street the voice of a hell-fire preacher denouncing Bill Haley, rock'n'roll, jazz, the cinema and their collective works and pomps.

Limerick had three local newspapers then. The *Limerick Leader*, owned by the Buckley family and edited by the aged and autocratic Con Cregan, was the biggest. Next—in status though not in circulation—came the *Limerick Chronicle*, soon to merge with the *Leader* but at this stage still under the control of the diminutive Paddy Fitzgibbon in its Dickensian office in O'Connell Street. The *Limerick Weekly Echo and District Advertiser* (known locally as the *Weekly Echo*) was controlled by the Morris brothers, who were Protestants, but its appeal was almost exclusively to working-class Roman Catholics. In a city where at that time a large section of the population regarded snobbishness as a civic duty it suffered because of its down-market image. For the sophisticates of Ballinacurra and the Ennis Road, to be seen with a copy of the *Weekly Echo* would be a social solecism as grievous as being caught using margarine instead of butter. Although it battled valiantly for years, it never succeeded in overtaking the *Leader* and eventually succumbed in the Eighties.

I look back on it and the lean-to with the greatest affection. Here I made my first friends in journalism: Frank Corr, the youthful advertising manager who soon changed over to journalism; Pat and John Finn, philosophers who took photographs and ran the Echo Photo Service; and the ebullient editor, who opened a door in journalism to me.

TP Morris, though he never had a formal training in journalism, was an excellent editor. Impervious to flattery, devoid of cant and humbug, he revelled in a show of philistinism in which everything had to be reduced to pence, shillings and pounds—and in that order. He was a Thatcherite before the lady from Grantham was even heard of, railing against the extravagances of local councils and the iniquities of bureaucracies and trade unions. He had a good eye for a story and an even better one for the till. He was constantly urging economies such as sending postcards rather than making trunk phone calls. "A postcard costs only tuppence," he always said.

Leaning over my shoulder one morning in August 1962 he asked: "Pray, what are we at now, Mr O'Toole?" I volunteered that I was writing the obituary of the Shakespearean actor, Anew McMaster, who had just died in Dublin. "Desist, Mr O'Toole!" cried the editor with the urgency of a woman who has just seen smoke coming out of the oven. "You can take the paper out of the typewriter this very instant and put it in the bin."

Thinking that the piece had offended merely against his dictum that "a dog fight in Ballynanty is more important than an earthquake in Ballyfermot," I pointed out that Anew McMaster had been well known in Limerick for his frequent appearances at the City Theatre and in parish halls throughout the county.

"I'm well aware of that to my cost, Mr O'Toole," said the boss. "The last time that gentleman appeared at the City Theatre he departed without paying for a six-inch double-column ad."

Tommy had little time for actors—Shakespearean or otherwise. It was far from Shakespeare, he insisted, that the concerns of the vast bulk of the *Echo*'s readership lay. He claimed that the most successful series of articles he ever published were written by a local man named JJ Hobbins and entitled: "How I Cured My Catarrh." The response had been so great that he later published them in booklet form. After I had mentioned Sean Lemass in my column he took me aside and said: "Sean Lemass stopped cutting articles about himself out of the paper years ago. Concentrate on the people whose names have never appeared in print before and who will rush out and buy five or six copies of the paper to send to their brothers and sisters in England. These are the people I want in the *Echo* and not Sean Lemass who probably doesn't even know of our existence."

By the time I got to know him he had more or less given up his fight to outsell the *Leader* and the paper was already in decline. He used to boast sometimes that when he and Ivan took over the *Echo* it had a circulation of minus six. "You can understand the plight of a man taking over a paper with a circulation of plus six," he would say stabbing the air with his pipe, "but weren't we two brave men to take one over with a circulation of minus six?" That peculiar situation came about because for a few weeks the previous proprietor printed only six copies which he sent out as voucher copies to contract advertisers.

Like many local papers in Ireland, the *Echo* was of secondary importance to the printing business that was carried out alongside. In some cases these papers existed solely to keep printers occupied in between jobbing business and the proprietors regarded the editorial matter as something to flush out the advertisements. In many cases journalistic standards were non-existent, the journalists concentrating on the reiteration of local myths and the production of cheap, safe copy most of which came from either the local courts or the county council. When a colleague got a job as editor of a now defunct local paper he was chuffed to find a good strong lead story for his first issue as editor. Returning from lunch on press day he found that his fine story had been removed from the page to make way for a large advertisement for a local draper. When he protested, it was explained that the proprietor's wife had done a barter deal whereby her two sons were kitted out for confirmation in consideration of the advertisement which had replaced the lead story.

Such conduct wouldn't have been countenanced at the *Echo*—the Morris brothers were too professional for that. But the paper eventually became bland and was concentrating too much on cures for catarrh and on homely little fillers provided (free) by Aims of Industry. At one stage the *Echo* had tried to tackle social issues but the Limerick of the 1940s and '50s wasn't ready for that kind of journalism.

John and Pat Finn had been freelancing for the *Evening Press*, specialising in pictures of decorous maidens with beehive hair-dos draped around settees at social functions in Cruise's and The Royal George. John worked through the night scouring the hotels in search of Limerick's fairest and demurest, departing in the early hours and leaving the film for Pat to process. Pat would arrive at around 10 am, develop the film and send the prints to Dublin.

John was a great man for logical thought and one day he said: "If the *Evening Press* take pictures from me, why shouldn't they take articles from you?" I promptly wrote a short piece and a few evenings later I opened the paper and there it was in all its loveliness. These short articles, known in the trade as "fillers" and "pre-fabs," were used in the news pages of early editions. They were typeset in quantity, stored in racks in the caseroom and shovelled in whenever there was a shortage of news. Then as real news materialised they were shovelled out again with equal rapidity. These pieces were regarded as pure dross but they were paid for at the rate of three guineas each and in the early 1960s that was generous. After my third or fourth piece had been published in the *Evening Press*, I decided it was time the hotel industry would have to learn to exist without me and I set myself up as a full-time freelance journalist.

As it turned out, this momentous and very foolish decision caused not a ripple in the catering industry, which continued to trundle on oblivious to its great loss. But the world of Limerick journalism was shaken to its very foundations.

In those days some Limerick journalists operated an informal cartel arrangement under which information was often pooled to minimise the danger of being scooped or, as journalists say, stuck. From the point of view of the journalists it was a sensible system which eliminated the danger of a 1am call from the newsdesk asking whether that exclusive in the opposition's first edition was accurate and please run a check and get on to copy with a re-jig within twenty minutes. It also offered insurance against the nightmare of being stuck on the really big story—the air crash, the whole family perishing in a house fire, the sudden death of the local government minister...

Clearly, I was going to threaten the status quo and, even more clearly, it was obvious that there was going to be a reaction. A couple of members of the Limerick press corps entered the fray and went to great lengths to have me discredited. One of them told a public meeting in Cruise's that I was "a kitchen hand from Shannon airport who aspires to journalism." Sometimes I found that invitations to cover functions were being withdrawn after the organisers had been approached and told that my presence might endanger coverage where it mattered. The excuse was the standard one—I wasn't a member of the NUJ. And the reason I wasn't in the NUJ was the classic Catch 22 which bedevils many a late entrant to journalism: you can't have an NUJ card unless through journalism you earn at least two-thirds of the minimum NUJ senior rate for the locality, and the NUJ will meanwhile do its damnedest to ensure that those who do not have NUJ cards earn nothing at all from journalism, let alone two-thirds of the local senior rate.

There is a widespread belief among the public that one cannot be a journalist unless one belongs to the NUJ. This fallacy has been carefully nurtured by many NUJ members and in the Limerick of the 1960s it had the status of holy writ. It is, of course, utter nonsense. The NUJ is no more than one of several trade unions for journalists that exist around the world. At that time there were three Congress-affiliated trade unions for journalists in Ireland: the National Union of Journalists (NUJ), the Institute of Journalists (IOJ) and the Guild of Irish Journalists (GIJ). The title National Union of Journalists is a misnomer, and membership is in itself no guarantee that one is a journalist at all. For me, the Guild of Irish Journalists, then on its last legs and long since defunct, was the escape hatch. It was in every legal sense as legitimate a trade union for journalists as the NUJ and it was happy to have me as a member.

It wasn't enough. The late Maxwell Sweeney, then editor of the *Irish Hotel and Catering Review*, assigned me to cover diploma day at the Shannon Hotel School. When I turned up at the luncheon the other journalists threatened to walk out. Jorgen Blum, the director of the school, was made of harder metal than the many local organisers who wilted at the first signs of pressure. Blum was an impatient man at the best of times and he had no interest in a dissertation on the subtleties of interrelations between Irish trade unions. To his blunt Swiss way of thinking a union card was a union card. And to my great relief he announced that as far as he was concerned I was a member of a journalists' trade union, I was representing a magazine which had been invited to cover the event and I was welcome to stay. Anyone who felt the need to leave because of that should feel free to do so. No one left.

It seems so unimportant now, yet on this trivial incident hung my whole career as a journalist. Jorgen Blum had no way of knowing that this was my Rubicon. My confidence

had almost been shattered and I was at the lowest ebb. Had
he turned me away then I doubt if I would have had the
stomach to try ever again. Nearly a quarter of a century
later, half way across the Pacific on a Pan Am clipper, the
whole incident came rushing back to me. I was reading for
the first time F Scott Fitzgerald's short story "Basil: the
Freshest Boy" and came upon the lines:

> It isn't given to us to know those rare moments when
> people are wide open and the lightest touch can wither or
> heal. A moment too late and we can never reach them
> any more in this world. They will not be cured by our
> most efficacious drugs or slain with our sharpest swords.

Sweet as it was, the victory was short-lived. It soon
became obvious to me that I wasn't going to be able to
make a living. Untrained, inexperienced, without resources
as I was, to try to earn a living as a journalist was like
trying to cross the Atlantic in a bath tub. I decided to try
my luck in London, which I knew well as I had done part
of my catering training there. Pat Comyn, the newly arrived
and approachable editor of the *Limerick Leader*, agreed to
let me write a column from London called "Limerickman's
Diary." The fee was minimal, but the column would at
least give me an entrée and perhaps pave the way towards
NUJ membership.

My exile was short. I spotted an advertisement for a
senior reporter in the head office of the *Leinster Leader*. And
while I doubted if someone of my meagre experience would
have much of a chance, I sent off my application and a few

days later I was summoned to the cold, self-assured town of Naas to be interviewed by Senan Carroll. Even though he was the *de facto* editor, because of an unhappy wrangle with a previous editor Senan was required to style himself sub-editor, the title of editor being invested in the managing director. To my great surprise, I was hired at what to me was the substantial wage of £18 a week. I've often wondered why Senan gave me the job. Although I was well able to put a story together and had a well-developed news sense, I was still inexperienced in most of the skills that were most vital to a sound local newspaper such as the *Leinster Leader*. I had only very limited experience of court coverage, I had no shorthand and I had never covered a county council or other local authority meeting. Add to this my total lack of local knowledge—a very severe handicap to even the most skilled reporter on a local paper—and my qualifications seemed paltry indeed. But I succeeded and I spent a very happy and worthwhile time in Naas. Years later my brother-in-law, Tony Browne, joined the *Leader* and took over my old beat.

Life on the *Leinster Leader* was civilised and tranquil. There was a small though comfortable newsroom where we sat like guests at a dinner party around a mahogany table. In winter a good coal fire blazed in the grate and every Friday morning Bill Britton, the managing director, would come up with the wage packets. The *Leinster Leader* was one of the country's leading printing houses. The paper was conservative, bland (in those days it carried no leading articles), reliable and accurate. It took care not to cause offence. For some strange reason it was known in Naas as the "Leinster Liar"—a sobriquet which no paper deserved less. The circulation area was divided into five sections with a staff reporter in charge of each. I was assigned to north Kildare, that luscious golden vale of the midlands which is wedged between greater Dublin to the east and the Offaly-Westmeath border to the west. Each Monday morning I set out from Naas to tour my territory and to call on our correspondents in the towns and villages along the way.

The role of the village press correspondent has diminished in recent years as the number of professional freelance journalists has grown. At one time this army of amateur reporters was the backbone of every local paper as they recorded, week in week out, the short and simple annals of the parish: births, holidaying emigrants, the first cuckoo, success at the SRN examinations, first snow on the mountain, oversize cabbages, deaths, grotesquely shaped potatoes, downed racing pigeons, weddings, Corpus Christi processions, bingo winners, appointments of peace commissioners, return of prodigal sons, old coins, religious professions, items dug up and prizes at horticultural shows— these and many other routine happenings have always been the raw materials of the local correspondent. Some like to mock this kind of reporting. They are fools who do so—it has a timelessness and a fascination that is universal.

My first call on Mondays was to Maynooth where our correspondent Gerry MacTernan held court in Phil Brady's lounge bar. Gerry was the ideal local correspondent: not only did he have a good news sense but he was a parish institution and involved in a huge range of activities from meals on wheels to the GAA. Nothing escaped him, and he had a genuine feel for village life in all its moods and subtleties. He was particularly assiduous in covering weddings, calling to the home of the bride to write down the details of the trousseau. He rated these weddings as "one-bottle," "two-bottle" or even "three-bottle" affairs, signifying the number of bottles of stout he had been treated to as he took down the details.

I sat in the press box at Naas district court listening to the mild and punctilious Justice Michael Keane preside over the reiteration of the misdemeanours of hundreds of miscreants. Across the corridor, the late Kenneth Deale of the circuit court dealt with more weighty matters. Mr Justice Deale—he was later elevated to the High Court—was at that time the only member of the Irish judiciary who wouldn't allow barristers or anyone else to address him as "my lord." Those who transgressed were courteously reproved and told that this was a republic and there were no lords here.

I wasn't exactly in love with Naas. I found it a cold place, physically and otherwise. There seemed to be more than the usual amount of small-town resentment of out-siders (in Naas outsiders were termed "whistlers") and my total indifference to horse-racing made me a kind of pariah in a society where people actually did bet on flies going up walls.

I had digs on the Kilcullen Road with a landlady who was suspicious of journalists and pined for the old days when she kept only banking gentlemen. She claimed to be subject to supernatural visitations and delighted in recounting these experiences. She was a splendid if slightly eccentric cook. It took me a while to work out that her method of portion control was based entirely on the diner's performance at the previous meal. If one ate only half one's breakfast then one would be penalised with an especially skimpy portion for lunch. Eventually she threw me and the other lodger out and I took off to the easygoing and kindly Mrs Burke in Our Lady's Place where I was very content indeed.

But I was bored. Then one morning I got a phone call from Pat Comyn of the *Limerick Leader*. He had a vacancy for a senior reporter. Would I like to come and see him? The stall warning should have sounded but it didn't. Lulled into a sense of false security by even a brief period in a civilised office where people got on with their jobs and had no use for intrigue and office politics, I failed to anticipate the fury that my return to Limerick would cause among certain elements of the journalistic establishment there. I told Pat Comyn I'd be delighted to come and see him, and walked blithely into a nightmare that would last for a whole year.

3

"MY DEAR NATIVE PLACE"

The past is a foreign country: they do things differently there.

LP Hartley, *The Go-Between*

In 1962, her creative talents largely spent, Kate O'Brien wrote a strange dedication to her travel book *My Ireland*. She had given up the practice of dedicating her books after 1934 when she inscribed her second novel, *The Ante Room*, to her sister, Nance, and her brother-in-law, Stephen O'Mara. Now, three decades on, she took up the practice again and wrote: "With warmest love, as my father Tom O'Brien would have thought proper, I humbly dedicate this little book to Limerick, my dear native place."

That Kate O'Brien should have written these lines in dedication of what was anything but a "little" book may itself be an indication of the detachment and generosity of that formidable lady. She was—and still is—Limerick's finest writer. The years in which her creative talents flowered coincided with the worst fevers of the great Irish censorship and, along with practically every other Irish writer of worth,

[38]

her work was banned.

In the city that she had presented to the world as Mellick, the odium of the official censorship was backed by rumour, innuendo and misrepresentation. Didn't everyone in the Limerick of the 1950s know that Reverend Mother FCJ had written from Laurel Hill to its former student asking why she was disgracing the convent by writing salacious books and that Miss O'Brien, the hussy, had replied with a mere postcard bearing an English stamp and containing only the words: "Pounds, shillings and pence." And so when it was suggested to the Limerick city council that the author of *Without My Cloak* and *The Land of Spices* should be given the freedom of the city the idea was promptly abandoned on the grounds that the clergy might make trouble.

Miss O'Brien kept her head in the air and refused to join that band of writers and journalists who down the years ensured that poor old Limerick got a consistently bad press. She would have none of this. It was in Limerick, she declared, that she "began to view the world and to develop the necessary passion by which to judge it. I know that wherever I am it is still from Limerick that I look out and make my surmises."

That's one thing I have in common with her. The other, as she took pains to point out on the one and only time I met her, is that she was a journalist. But her journalism was very different to mine—in her heyday she was the principal reviewer of fiction for *The Spectator*—and I doubt if she ever saw the inside of a police court. Her critical journalism, though, was both serious and generous and its philosophy is expressed in a couple of lines from her review of Elizabeth Coxhead's biography of Lady Gregory:

> Let us return for our own sakes to the lady of Coole and study her again—learn from her to be serious in art, to be humble, and to be generous towards talent as she always was—generous, instead of eternally malicious as it is often our curse to be.

Limerick was the first city I knew and its streets and alleys will always be magic places to me. Unlike Kate O'Brien, who was born in an imposing if ugly villa on the outskirts of the city, my own infinitely more humble birthplace was seventeen miles south east in the Golden Vale past Ballyneety, where—or so we Limerick folk like to think—Patrick Sarsfield delivered that great stroppy line to the Williamites: "Sarsfield is the word—and Sarsfield is the man."

This is important territory. Close by is Lough Gur, where men lived and farmed in the neolithic period, say around 3000 BC. A little to the south again is Knockainey ("the land sacred to Aine"), and my own village of Hospital is one of its suburbs, having being named after a thirteenth-century foundation of the Knights Hospitallers of St John of Jerusalem known as "the hospital at Any." On the way to Limerick you pass the ruins of Ballinagarde House, where the squire, John Croker, terminally ill but still with hunting horn in hand and his hounds around him, had the answer pat for his clergyman son when he suggested that he resign himself to abandoning the chase as greater joys soon awaited him:

> He tried to persuade him to make him resigned,
> On heavenly mansions to fasten his mind;
> "There's a land that is fairer than this you'll regard"—
> "I doubt it," says Croker of Ballinagarde.

And then, on a leafy stretch, the spire of St John's Cathedral—still the tallest church spire in Ireland—comes into view and soon the sounds and the smells of the city are all around you.

The opportunity of returning to practise my craft in "my dear native place" was immensely attractive. The new and youthful editor of the *Limerick Leader*, Pat Comyn, had been supportive when I was trying to break into journalism and I had written two regular columns for him on a freelance basis. He was now, he told me, assembling a team which would transform the stodgy old *Leader* and establish it as a modern-day version of the *Manchester Guardian*.

But the notion of implanting the liberal journalistic ideals of CP Scott on the Limerick of the 1960s was, at the very least, naïve. The Limerick of those days was a different world from the city of today. There was no university; unemployment was high and an inordinate proportion of the jobs were in low-paid service industries. Artistic endeavour, such as it was, was largely amateurish and desultory, and an overpowering sense of Jansenistic religiosity permeated the entire city. Brendan Behan, on a brief visit, had inelegantly described the place as "the city of piety and shiety." The all-powerful Redemptorist archconfraternity—then the largest body of its kind in the world—was still a huge influence with its members, their sashes and medals gleaming, marching Orange-Order style to church behind brass bands and banners. In those days the confraternity members gave the straight-hand fascist salute to their spiritual director. No one has ever been able to explain to me how this salute came to be adopted by a religious body.

The Redemptorist confraternity had a huge influence over the *Limerick Leader*, as did the Knights of St Columbanus, whose two local councils (CK 39 and 90) had a direct entrée to the paper through the then general manager, Jimmy Kelly, a leading member of the organisation. In addition to being general manager, Kelly took a keen interest in the editorial affairs of the paper and contributed a weekly comment column under the pseudonym "Spartacus."

The influence of the Redemptorists on the entire culture of Limerick has been enormous and will, I hope, provide some young social historian of the new University of Limerick with a fascinating PhD thesis. Founded in Naples in the mid-eighteenth century with the specific objective of caring for "the most abandoned souls," the Redemptorists arrived in Limerick in 1852 as part of Cardinal Cullen's "devotional revolution" to re-evangelise the Irish. Limerick had not been their first choice—the Redemptorist superiors had hoped for a foundation in Dublin—but Cullen craftily diverted them to Limerick, where he rightly assumed that the competition provided by a body of zealous, no-nonsense pulpit-thumpers would put manners on the established and relaxed Dominicans and Franciscans who were now seen to have become lax. As underdogs are wont to do, the Redemptorists eagerly set themselves to the task of establishing themselves as the dominant men in their field—in their case the hell, fire and brimstone business. And they succeeded most brilliantly.

The Redemptorists concentrated their Methodist-style evangelism largely on the working classes, leaving the salvation of the bourgeoisie to the Jesuits down the road at The Crescent. In Kate O'Brien's fictional works it is the Jesuit fathers and the nuns of the Compagnie de la Sainte Famille (the model for the FCJs) whom we meet rather than the Redemptorists and the sisters of the Presentation. In *The Ante Room* when on the Eve of All Saints Agnes Mulqueen presents herself to be shriven of the sin of coveting her sister's husband, it is to the Crescent rather than to Mount St Alphonsus that she is driven and the letters after the confessor's name are SJ rather than CSsR. Spiritual comforts can be as rigidly graded as temporal ones.

In journalism the Redemptorists exercised a subtle influence through individual reporters who were in awe of them and whom they skilfully manipulated. Gerry Ryan, then chief reporter of the *Leader*, would automatically phone the director of the confraternity on press day respectfully asking whether there was anything he wanted put into the paper. This privilege didn't stretch to the other denominations. On my first day in the *Leader* Gerry handed me the current issue of the *Church of Ireland Gazette* saying with obvious distaste: "Have a look at this ould Protestant thing and see if there's anything in it."

And it wasn't only in the local press that the Redemptorists were given sway over what the citizens might or might not read or view. The local repertory company, The College Players, employed the Redemptorists as unofficial censors on the understanding that it was open to them to excise any line or lines that might be considered unsuitable. A number of Redemptorists would attend each dress rehearsal and afterwards confer with the producer of the play.

When I joined the *Limerick Leader* in 1963 the confraternity was enjoying the last years of its mass popularity and was still capable of mounting campaigns to preserve local morality. In these it found an enthusiastic partner in the *Leader*. One of the last of these campaigns, in the mid-1950s, was against alleged immorality in Limerick city cinemas. Like the other campaigns it was based on either imaginary or totally inflated notions of what was going on. It attracted international publicity and helped reinforce the image of Limerick as a city of religious bigots and fanatics.

With its high population of young and poorly paid workers, Limerick always had a big cinema trade. The cinema, along with the weekend hop, was the only cheap form of public entertainment which embraced both sexes. Despite the existence of an official censor, the confraternity had always been suspicious of the cinema and, on at least one occasion, had organised the public burning of a film which it considered unsuitable for Limerick minds and consciences. The mid-Fifties was a time of extreme religious fanaticism in Ireland, particularly in regard to entertainment.

The ballroom industry had been thrown into chaos after wild rumours that a young woman had fled in hysterics from a dance hall in the west after espying the devil's cloven hoof protruding from the right trouser-leg of her partner. Indeed, the reports went on to claim that the same cloven hoof had left its fiery imprints on the dance floor for all to see. This was followed up by a Redemptorist pamphlet, *The Devil at Dances*, which became a bestseller. (Devil imagery was a main plank of Roman Catholic propaganda in the 1950s. An article of the period, "Satan and the Silver Screen" by Seamus Hurley, SVD in a Catholic magazine is illustrated with a drawing of a film director with cloven hooves and horns looking through a cine-camera.)

Now the word went round that "immoral practices" were taking place in the back seats of city cinemas and the confraternity soon became engulfed in an imaginary sea of illicit sex. Vigilantes were appointed to patrol the cinemas and to report back to the director. The story travelled round the world—even *The Spectator* commented on the imaginary depravities of the youth of Limerick.

The last great public morality campaign of the confraternity was fought in 1963, the year I joined the staff of the *Limerick Leader*. It started with the publication in the *Leader* of a letter complaining that books with "filthy pictures" were being sold in city shops. The letter bore the pseudonym "Terrified" and it was followed by several others in similar vein, practically all of them under pseudonyms. Several letters suggested that vigilantes should be appointed to inspect bookshops and newsagents. The confraternity was immediately involved and its director assisted the vigilantes in calling on bookshops, newsagents and libraries. An attempt was made to revive the cinemas campaign and weary cinema workers were called to a series of late-night meetings at Connolly Hall where they were lectured on their responsibilities to the upkeep of a proper standard of public morality. A poem (in Italian) found in a public library was denounced as lewd, and a dealer in second-hand books appeared in the District Court accused of having four banned books on his premises. (The titles were: *Cabbage Holiday*, *The Wind that Shakes the Barley*, *Arctic Village* and *Mr Stimpson and Mr Gorse*.) Justice de Burca accepted the defence that the dealer having bought his stock in lots of 500 was unaware that the books had been banned, and he applied the Probation of Offenders Act.

On Saturday, 2 February, 1963, the *Limerick Chronicle* (sister paper of the *Leader*) carried the banner headline: "Adults Not Immune to Evil Books—Preacher Outlines Church Attitude." Alongside a three-column picture of the confraternity director, Fr Gerard Mahon, was the text of his sermon. The Church, Fr Mahon said, was wiser in her judgements than the so-called children of light.

The experience of the centuries has taught her, sorrowfully, that countless numbers have read themselves out of their faith and into lives of error and sin...

Those who carp at the Church's laws with regard to forbidden literature seem to be unaware that the prohibition to read certain literature is a very ancient practice and was in use even before the Christian era. It was in vogue among the Jews before the Babylonian captivity. According to the pagan historian Livy, it was the duty of magistrates in the early days of the Roman Empire to forbid literature that was in any way harmful to the citizens...

The *Leader* was even harder on the "so-called children of light" than Fr Mahon. One leading article of the campaign began: "One of the most frequent and what is contended to be one of the most scathing indictments of this country by the so-called intelligentsia is our Censorship Board. The work of that body is seen as a method of stifling all worthwhile creative literature and of sending our best writers to earn international reputations abroad. Even if these criticisms were well founded, they could not be weighted in the balance against the possibility, indeed the probability, of Irish readers becoming contaminated by books and magazines not alone superficially undesirable but foul in the extreme..."

There was, of course, no organised trade in pornography in Limerick in 1963 any more than there was widespread promiscuity in the back seats at the Savoy or the Lyric. The confraternity was having one of its periodic bouts of hysteria and it was being aided and abetted by a large section of the local press. But, unlike the earlier and more notorious campaign of violence and vilification against the city's tiny Jewish community, no bones were broken on this occasion. In fact, to most of those under fifty the 1963 campaign was a bit of a joke. Not long afterwards Fr Mahon left the Redemptorists and the priesthood.

Practically all editors of local papers come up through the ranks in provincial journalism and, more often than not, succeed to the editorship of the paper where they started. Our editor, Pat Comyn, was an exception. Trained on the *Drogheda Independent,* he soon moved to the *Irish Press* and later to the *Irish Independent* working exclusively as a sub-editor on the two Dublin papers. He was—and still is, I'm sure—a most accomplished professional sub with the ability to shift even the rawest copy at record speed. His technical abilities greatly improved the appearance of the *Leader* and its circulation steadily increased under his editorship. But improving the design of a newspaper is a simple matter in comparison to changing its policy and content. Pat Comyn didn't stay long in Limerick and by the time he left to join Aer Lingus as a public relations executive the *Leader* was still as remote from CP Scott's *Manchester Guardian* as the *Dandy* was from *The Times.* It is no criticism of Pat Comyn that this should be so. No editor—not even Scott himself—could have swung the *Leader* round to liberal, independent thinking at that particular point of its history.

My year on the staff of the *Limerick Leader* was dramatically bitter-sweet. It was to include one of the most painful experiences of my life, and in some ways I bear the scars of it still. On the other hand it was to bring me great happiness for which I will always be grateful. It included intrigue, tyranny, falling in love and the cementing of friendships that have endured down the years.

Even though I was relatively naïve in those days, it was immediately obvious to me that my arrival in the *Leader* newsroom wasn't exactly sending my colleagues into paroxysms of delight and enthusiasm. Pat Comyn was most welcoming and friendly but the others, in the main, were just coolly polite. And one person, the news editor, was actively hostile.

Tom Tobin had been appointed news editor on the day I joined the *Leader*. He had come to the paper through the Shannon Free Airport Development Company where he had worked as a press officer. He came originally from Dungarvan, Co Waterford, and specialised in melodramatic feature articles of great length. Two of his favourite themes were Crotty the robber, a famous bandit of the Comeragh Mountains, and Little Nellie of Holy God, a tragic and consumptive orphan whose great piety had been brought to the attention of Pope Pius X. He wrote a comment column for the paper under the pseudonym "Vigilans" and—although this wasn't generally realised at the time— he had a searing ambition—ultimately realised—to occupy the editorial chair. Unfortunately, he saw me as a threat to that ambition. It was one of his many ill-founded judgements for I never, either then or since, did aspire to being editor of a newspaper.

Tom was determined not only to get me out of the *Leader* but also to have me expelled from the NUJ and, consequently, out of journalism. He waged a continuous battle on both fronts, winning the first and losing the second by the narrowest of margins. He marked me for every lousy assignment that turned up. He saw to it that I was given an inordinate amount of late-evening work. He ridiculed and denigrated my work and tried to prevent other members of the staff from associating with me. More lethal still, he invented a whole series of bogus assignments which I never knew about but which he passed on to the management with reports that I had either refused to go on them or failed to produce copy. The concept of natural justice wasn't as much in vogue then as it is now and it certainly doesn't appear to have permeated the boardroom of the *Limerick Leader* because I was never once given the opportunity of defending myself against these false charges.

Tom's opportunity to deliver the *coup de grâce* came when I obliged him with a serious slip-up in reporting a court case. While I was filing copy at the Limerick district court a garda whom I knew approached me about a small case in which he had been involved and which had been heard while I was out of the courtroom. He was doing the sergeants' exam in a couple of weeks and a mention would be most helpful. If he gave me the details would I oblige with a paragraph?

I duly obliged and did what no reporter should ever do but which, nevertheless, was sometimes done in those less litigious days—base even the briefest court report on details obtained from an official without inspecting the court documents. In my case the resultant error couldn't have been more nightmarish—the names of the defendant and the injured party had become transposed. Nothing happened to us, but another country paper that had "lifted" the item had to apologise and, I think, pay a small sum to a charity.

My sacking was crudely executed. That Friday I was in the district court as usual when Tony Purcell, then the office junior, arrived breathless and whey-faced to the press box. He had been sent to take over from me, he explained, and I was to report immediately to the office. Everyone knew except me.

There had been a board meeting that morning but it fell to Pat Comyn to deliver the bad news. He was sympathetic and advised me to get myself another job quietly rather than risk publicity by going to an appeals tribunal.

I was devastated and my options were few. Still perilously inexperienced as a journalist, I had neither money nor influence. Although there had been a softening of attitude towards me by some of my *Limerick Leader* colleagues, most of what passed for the journalistic establishment in Limerick still regarded me as an interloper and a charlatan. As well as exercising considerable power in the *Limerick Leader*, Tom Tobin was a major force in the local branch of the NUJ. Eventually, after intervention by the NUJ's newly appointed national organiser, Jim Eadie, a deal was done. The notice was withdrawn, and I resigned and got another job in Burgh Quay.

Even after all these years the *Leader* experience chills me whenever I think about it. It happened at a time when I was particularly vulnerable and it almost destroyed my confidence in myself as a journalist. But it did have a positive side to it. It developed in me an unquenchable loathing of the petty tyrannies of aspiring dictators and tinpot ayatollahs everywhere, be they trade-union bosses, clerics or newspaper editors. It also reinforced in me the very definite feeling of always being an outsider. And that is no bad thing for a journalist.

But of course there is another set of memories of Limerick that always supersedes the bad ones, memories that principally concern the *Leader*'s first woman reporter, Maureen Browne, and my first friends in journalism, Frank Corr of the *Limerick Weekly Echo*, and John and Pat Finn of the *Echo Photo Service*. "Pat Finn," as our astute licensed vintner, Willie Gleeson, once observed, "is a fine decent man—but John is a superior type." Pat and I put down many a pint in Willie's Sarsfield Street hostelry (now Riddlers) while the prints were washing in Pat's darkroom across the road. Pat eventually drifted out of photography. He never, I think, quite recovered from missing, directly on his doorstep, what he claimed would have made the outstanding features picture of the decade. A flock of sheep being driven down Henry Street to a nearby slaughterhouse stampeded into the Franciscan church and ran amok in the pews. A friar who obviously hadn't been blessed with his holy founder's devotion to dumb animals grabbed a processional pole bearing a picture of St Anthony and with a most unFranciscanlike ferocity proceeded to beat the sheep on to the street. Pat, emerging from Willie's, observed the figure of the friar framed in the church door, his staff poised for another belt, and the terrified sheep leaping all over the place. Pat was so disgusted at the fact that he had no camera that he turned and went back into the pub.

I don't suppose I would ever have succeeded in journalism if it weren't for Frank Corr's encouragement and friendship. Frank's infectious enthusiasm and sense of fun have in no way been tarnished by the years. He left

Limerick a few years after me and came to Dublin to work in *Business and Finance*. After that he moved to Jemma Publications, where he is editorial director.

That steadfast man, Jim Kemmy, was another friend of those *Leader* days. Like me, Jim had recently returned from exile in London and was already establishing his political base. He had just founded his paper, the *Limerick Socialist* which, come rain or shine, he sold, price sixpence, at street corners. He was aware of my difficulties at the *Leader* and, not surprisingly, counselled perseverance—one of the characteristics which has marked his own political career. Even though as I grew older I came to regard socialism as a flawed and suspect political system, my admiration for Jim Kemmy has never waned. I see him as being in the mould of some of the great early English socialists: doughty, democratic, fair-minded, genuinely interested in the advancement of the underprivileged, modest in lifestyle and concerned with the things of the intellect. His contribution to Limerick has been enormous and ranges from his fine restoration work in St John's Square (Jim is a stone-mason by trade) to the establishment of the splendid *Old Limerick Journal*, which he edits.

Maureen Browne caused something of a sensation when she joined the staff soon after me. When he announced her impending arrival Pat Comyn asked for decorum in the newsroom, particularly in regard to language. His concern, he soon discovered, was entirely misplaced. Ms Browne turned out to be a tough nut who was determined to get away from the safe subjects that most women reporters concentrated on in those days. It soon became apparent that here was the makings of a very fine hard-news reporter, and so, indeed, it turned out.

She was from Bruff; I was from Hospital, five miles over the road. That gave us something of an affinity. Besides, she soon spotted that I was being given a raw deal and if Maureen has a weakness it is in her sympathy for the underdog. After work we would take a bundle of newspapers, Irish and English, over to her flat in Catherine Street and pore over them for hours comparing story with story, headline with headline. We were both enthusiastic learners and there is no better way of learning about journalism than by reading the papers.

On payday we would eat in the Brazen Head, then The Talk of the Town grill in The Savoy and, as the week wore on and the money got scarcer, we would dine on fish and chips in the Café Capri. (It was in the Café Capri that we decided to get married.) On Thursdays, if Gerry Kennedy, who was in charge of the payroll, couldn't be found to advance a loan, Maureen would remove the threepenny-bits which in those pre-tights days invariably kept up her stockings, and buy a few sausages in the Catherine Street Dairy. A few months after I left the *Leader* she too got a job in Burgh Quay, where she soon established a reputation as an outstanding member of the news team. Maureen comes of a farming background and three of the four children went into journalism. Two married journalists (Bette, now with Reuters in New York, married another *Irish Press* reporter, Tom O'Connor.) When our son Feargal was little he thought everyone in the world worked in newspapers. Now he is training for the old black art himself. Our daughter, Orla, has no interest in journalism and is a teacher of Irish. Our youngest, Justin, is the only member of the family to share my interest in aviation. He wants to be a pilot.

Limerick has changed completely since my brief spell there as a reporter. It has always had a bad press but the charges of coldness and unfriendliness have been exaggerated. As so often happens in journalism, certain clichés become fashionable and in the case of Limerick whole generations of journalists have approached it with preconceived notions and never gave it a fair chance. Even in my time there was always more to laugh about than to cry about; true there were bigots aplenty but there was never a shortage of decent warmhearted souls always ready to burst into chat or into song. And you didn't have to be a rugby *aficionado* to share in that camaraderie although if you were it certainly helped. Limerick has at last come of age. More than any living person, its mayor, Jim Kemmy, has seen to that. Its university and urban restoration programme have given it new confidence, the kind of confidence that Kate O'Brien would have wished for it. She regarded Limerick as a "representative" city for Ireland and she took her bearings for life from it.

4

THIS GREAT ENTERPRISE

Our intention is to be the voice of the people, to speak for them, to give utterance to their ideals, to defend them against slander and false witness.

Irish Press, 5 September, 1931 (first leading article)

Surviving its birth was the first major miracle of the *Irish Press*. Vilified by the establishment, undercapitalised, bludgeoned by powerful and ruthless competitors and staffed by what its first editor charitably described as "the most mixed elements," it made its first appearance on Saturday, 5 September, 1931.

In the early days de Valera liked to refer to it as "this great enterprise" and he went on the record that if forced to choose between the party and the paper he would opt for the paper. The other work, he told the 1931 Fianna Fáil Ard-Fheis, could go on without him but the work of the *Irish Press* was of supreme importance at the present time.

The *Irish Press* would not, its first leading article insisted, be "the organ of an individual or a group, or a party..." It would, of course, support the Fianna Fáil party—but only because the philosophy and aspirations of Fianna Fáil were identical with its own philosophy and aspirations.

The *Irish Press* was not owned by the party and it would certainly not be controlled by it. The articles of association of *Irish Press* Ltd made that very clear. There would be a controlling director, the articles said, who "shall have sole and absolute control of the public and political policy of the Company and of the editorial management thereof... He may appoint and at his discretion remove or suspend all editors, sub-editors, reporters, writers, contributors of news and information, and all such other persons as may be employed in or connected with the editorial department..."

The notion of founding a newspaper that would be "national" in every sense of the term had been in de Valera's mind since 1922 when the Republican director of publicity said to him in a letter that if they could "break down the conspiracy of silence in the daily press" it would be worth ten times what they were doing in handbills. The Republican ideal had taken root without the assistance of any national daily newspaper and throughout the war of independence the British authorities received solid backing from these papers. The treaty had the solid support of the *Irish Independent* and the Unionist *Irish Times* accepted it with tolerant contempt. This was the era of the "mosquito press," a series of illegal publications, the most famous of which was the *Irish Bulletin*, official organ of the banned Dáil.

De Valera's original plan was to buy the *Freeman's Journal*, then in financial difficulties. This plan was scuppered by the industrialist William Martin Murphy, who acquired the paper and merged it with his *Irish Independent.* Then in December 1927 de Valera set off for the US on the first of his missions to raise funds for the venture in the land of his birth.

The American shares which ultimately allowed de Valera and his descendants, as trustees, to exercise total control over the company were to become an issue of great controversy and remain so to this day. The share capital for the new paper was set at £200,000 and it was planned to raise half of this in America from shareholders who would contribute a minimum of $500 each. De Valera's two-month tour of the US in 1927 failed to bring in the necessary £100,000. He went back again in 1929, staying this time for six months and setting up a network of fund-raising committees. By now the great recession was biting and again the target was far from met. De Valera now moved to get American holders of Republican bonds, subscribed a decade earlier and frozen by an American court because of a wrangle between the pro- and anti-treaty factions as to who owned the money, to invest their holdings. The *Irish Press* Corporation was set up and a sizeable number of bond-holders (the precise number has never been made public) converted their bonds into *Irish Press* shares. A trustee and representative of these share-holders on the *Irish Press* board was Eamon de Valera and this, combined with his own shareholding, gave him control of the company.

Even with the help of the US bonds, the company was severely undercapitalised. Despite showing a brave public face, de Valera was worried. Writing to a supporter in July

1931, he wrote: "The first year in its life is bound to be a critical one. I wish we had more reserve capital than we have. Except for anxiety on this point, I am full of hope that we shall win through, despite the desperate competition of our rivals."

The competitors were, indeed, desperate. It isn't easy across the divide of sixty years to appreciate the antipathy, the sheer fury even, with which the establishment viewed the prospect of a national newspaper controlled by Eamon de Valera. To many it was about the equivalent of Sinn Féin gaining control of Radio Éireann. In an age in which the chief power groupings of society—government, church and business—exercised a far greater control over the media than they now do, the possibility of such a powerful instrument falling into the hands of a man who was to varying degrees still regarded with suspicion by all of them was a grim prospect indeed.

As the launch date approached, de Valera abandoned practically all his political work in order to concentrate on his "great enterprise." The American trips had been used not only to collect money but to study newspaper technology and management. De Valera threw himself into the work with such minute attention to detail that his managers and journalists were driven almost to distraction. He insisted on mastering even the most arcane technicalities. His grandson, Eamon de Valera, who would succeed him as head of the venture, recalls how his grandfather amused him as a child by spreading large sheets of paper on the floor at Áras an Uachtaráin and, though almost totally blind, demonstrating how a printing press folded the paper into newspaper shape.

The mechanics of newspaper production continued to fascinate him. Ted Nealon, the journalist and Fine Gael TD, recalls an election campaign in Clare in the 1950s when he and some fellow reporters approached de Valera of a Saturday morning to inform him that unless they could get an advance dictate of that evening's speech it wouldn't, for logistical reasons, make the Sunday papers. De Valera, who on election campaigns made up his speeches as he travelled from one venue to the next, dutifully obliged with a speech on some topical national issue. On the night the reporters were alarmed to hear him address a different topic entirely and they sent up a note to remind him that the Sunday papers were already rolling with his original piece. De Valera read the note but he didn't change the topic. Instead he treated the bemused Clare audience standing around the lorry to an expert dissertation on the exigencies of Sunday newspaper production.

Paddy Clare, the paper's gravel-voiced night reporter for nearly fifty years and one of the "mixed elements" that the first editor spoke of, was on duty in the newsroom on the night of the first publication. Paddy recalled that he had never set out to join the *Irish Press*—he had no real journalistic training—and had merely wandered down Burgh Quay out of curiosity to see how the conversion of the Tivoli was progressing. He was looking through the window when a former colleague in arms from the Republican movement spotted him, summoned him in and immediately set him to work. Apart from a brief sabbatical which he spent fighting against Franco's forces in the Spanish civil war, Paddy remained with the firm for almost half a century.

In a short article on the fiftieth anniversary of the paper Paddy recalled the hectic days leading up to the launch. "People were ringing up at all hours to find out when the paper would be out, if ever. Up to the last minute some people had doubts about it. In the meantime there was much coming and going. A lot of Americans had contributed to the founding of the paper and Yanks and Southerners were continually calling in, all bringing good wishes. Some I remember well. There was one who called himself Brian Boru O'Dunne, and another character called Rory O'Moore Sarsfield...All sorts of things were being said: they [the Free Staters] wouldn't let it come out...It wouldn't last a month...One politician said it would suit Mr de Valera better to rebuild the tenement houses in Cumberland Street than starting this nonsense."

When the great night arrived it was Patrick Pearse's mother who pressed the button that started the presses. Paddy joined the exodus to the basement to witness the historic moment but was stopped in his tracks by Robert Egan, the news editor, who told him to stay in the newsroom and answer the phone. That, Paddy wrote, was the last straw. "I was not going to be deprived of this great moment, no, not me. I did something then that I have often done since—I lifted all the phones off the hooks and left them that way. I ran down to the basement and hid in the crowd behind Mr Egan. There was hardly room for a mouse to get a look in, people seemed to be everywhere...

We waited for a long time for the front page to come from the foundry, and then finally the plate was locked on to the rotary press and the signal was given.

"I heard the faint voice of a woman—it was probably Mrs Pearse speaking before pressing the button; then a sort of uneasy moment was felt around the assembly. Something, I felt, was bound to go wrong. We waited and I watched the great press for signs of movement. We had waited so long for this moment and now there was a hitch. But no, the press was slowly moving, too slow, I thought. And then a little bit faster and after about half a minute it really began to move and in a few moments was roaring madly...everyone was cheering and clapping...all around me people were waving and shouting as if the impossible was happening, and it was..."

Publicising the new paper had been a major problem as neither the *Irish Independent* nor *The Irish Times* would accept advertisements announcing the birth of a rival. De Valera had to rely on handbills, advertisements in local papers and on all-important word-of-mouth publicity directed through the Fianna Fáil cumainn network. Not all newspapers were hostile. Several months before the launch, the Irish correspondent of *The Sunday Times*, Sir John Keane, wrote the kind of puff that sends PR executives into ecstasies:

Fianna Fáil is to start a daily newspaper. This leaked out from the secret session of the Ard-Fheis, and the names of the board have been published. The capital proposed is £200,000 and it is hoped that a large proportion will be produced in America. The board is certainly impressive and seems to support the statement that the project is not too rigidly one of party. With the exception of Mr de Valera himself, who incidentally has considerable organising ability, all the directors are business men, and two are managing directors of successful companies. With a good management the project has every prospect of success, and if the circulation bears any relation to the party vote it ought to be considerable. There is ample scope for three daily papers, and the project ought to be generally welcome.

There was another vital constituency—the 8,000 small shareholders spread through the country providing, as de Valera said, "a representative practically in every parish." Three days before the launch, signing himself "do chara, Eamon de Valera," the founder wrote to each shareholder urging them to action and setting out how he wished them to promote the paper.

The Irish people, he wrote, were being provided with a daily newspaper "that will have no interests to serve but their interests. Each shareholder is a proprietor in the concern. The *Irish Press* is his paper. It is through his co-operation that it has been brought into existence. His money is invested in it. Its interests are his interests. The management will endeavour to make the paper one that every shareholder can be proud of. Let each show his pride in it, and uphold it in his district by word and by deed. The coming six months will be the most critical period for the enterprise. It is the period when those who are not with us will be against us. It is the period when co-operation by the shareholders with the management will be of especial value..."

He then set out three practical means by which the shareholders could help.

1: By immediately notifying your newsagent that you will be a regular purchaser of the paper, and by urging your friends and neighbours to enter into a similar engagement.

2: By giving the paper the advertising of your business and by securing for it the advertising of your friends and neighbours' business.

3: By taking as many further shares as possible in *Irish Press* Ltd, so that the whole of the authorised capital may be quickly available; and by informing your friends and neighbours that shares in *Irish Press* Ltd can still be secured—all shares to be fully paid for on application at the rate of £1 per share.

At home in Hospital, Co Limerick, my grandfather and namesake would have received one of these circulars. He was very definitely one of Dev's men, and when the *Irish Press* representative came to Hospital during that traumatic winter of 1929, he ignored the omens of the Wall Street crash and put himself down for five pounds. The fiver would have represented a considerable sacrifice to a man who had a large family and who was trying to make his way in a world which was far more hostile to the underdog than today's.

Looking down the faded page in the shareholders'

register that bears his name, I find under the heading "description of the allottees" that the good people of Hospital who subscribed to the chief's "great enterprise" that day included a newsagent, three farmers, two "ladies," three "married women," nine "gentlemen," one member of the county council, one Catholic curate and one BA. The smallest allotments (four instances) was five shares; seven shareholders took ten shares; five took fifty, and the largest shareholding, one of a hundred shares, was taken by the MCC (Member of the County Council).

I had been working in the *Irish Press* for at least a year before I discovered that my grandfather had been one of the small shareholders. Like every other journalist I had known in Burgh Quay, I had been hired without any reference to my political credentials. No one, politician or otherwise, had "put in a word" on my behalf. Because of my limited experience at that time, it is unlikely that any other national newspaper would have given me a job. I was hired purely because Sean Ward, then the news editor of the *Evening Press*, believed I showed promise and, since there was a shortage of journalists due to the development of RTE, I was at least as good as they could get.

I have always been proud of the fact that my family has been associated with the paper since its foundation, and I later increased the number of shares from five to 350. Sometimes during the AGM of the company when an old and often enfeebled veteran of the shareholders gets up and with all the indignation he (or more often she) can muster up starts to lambast the chairman about the paper going down the road to Sodom and Gomorrah while Mr de Valera turns in his grave, I amuse myself by thinking of my grandfather reading Dev's letter on the morning of Thursday, 3 September, 1931.

I see him standing by the fireplace in the little room off the tiny shop where, in the evenings, my grandmother would sit waiting for customers. "Each shareholder is a proprietor in the concern...The *Irish Press* is his paper...His money is invested in it...Its interests are his interests..." This illusion of ownership, of fellowship with the chief would have appealed to him, as it already had to the thousands who rallied to Fianna Fáil. He probably didn't know that de Valera had modelled this technique of bonding on that of Daniel O'Connell; that he prized even the tiniest financial commitment as the greatest guarantee of the sense of belonging which was so vital to any enterprise of this kind. Grandfather would probably have read the letter twice, well satisfied by the cordiality of the chairman of the board in signing himself "do chara." He might even have folded it carefully and put it in his waistcoat pocket to show to them in Canty's. He would follow its instructions carefully in the only way he could— by buying the paper and urging others to buy it. Extra shares were out of the question, and he had nothing to advertise. But he dutifully placed an order at EJ Mitchell's and bought and read the *Irish Press* every day for the thirty-odd years that were left to him.

In 1931 the *Irish Press* was both radical and rumbustious. By the nature of things it was always more radical and rumbustious when de Valera was out of government, and in 1931 he hadn't yet tasted power. In presentation as well as in content (it was the first national newspaper in Ireland to carry news on the front page) it differed radically from what was already on offer. The Limerick historian, Dr Mainchin Seoighe, remembers the excitement of the arrival of the first copy in his house. "As youngsters we got great enjoyment out of the serial *The Turf Cutter's Children* by Patricia Lynch, and the column by 'Roddy the Rover' (in real life Aodh de Blacam) was, I imagine, the best loved column ever to appear in an Irish newspaper," he wrote. "I remember neighbours who used visit our house at night frequently spending considerable time discussing what Roddy had written that day or the day before."

Another Roddy the Rover fan was Cardinal Tomás Ó Fiaich. "I remember what a thrill it always was to find that places we knew so well, like Creggan and Glasdrummond and Dorsey and Slieve Gullion, mentioned by him." My friend Con Houlihan, who as a columnist was to attain unprecedented popularity and become a similar cult figure in the *Evening Press*, claims that he was taught to read by his mother who used Roddy the Rover articles as texts. (At the party in Mulligan's for the relaunch of the *Irish Press* as a tabloid, Con, almost in tears, was railing against what he described as the desecration of a once great newspaper and cursing those responsible. At the height of this tirade the chairman and editor-in-chief, Eamon de Valera, joined our company. "What do you think of the new product," he asked Con innocently holding up the offending item. In what must rate as one of the finest ever examples of Kerry diplomacy, Con looked up and said: "Oh,'tis magic... magic..."

Its journalistic style and verve was more or less the creation of one remarkable man, Frank Gallagher, who edited it for the first four years and then, exhausted physically and mentally, and fearing that commercial considerations were eroding journalistic standards, made the supreme sacrifice by resigning.

He was a Cork man, born in that city in 1897 and in his teens apprenticed as a reporter to the *Cork Free Press*. His talent was immediately obvious and he was dispatched to London to cover the historic debates on Home Rule from the press gallery of the Westminster parliament. After 1916 he joined the Volunteers and was immediately caught up in the Republican propaganda machine of the time. He served under the Republican director of publicity, Erskine Childers—who became his hero—and played a big role in the operation of the mosquito press which flourished throughout the period of the Anglo-Irish war. As an editor he was a workaholic, a perfectionist, and something of a pedant who found it hard to delegate. He was also high-principled and intensely loyal to his staff as well as to the proprietor. The incident which ultimately caused him to resign was the dismissal of a staff member which he regarded as unjust. As far as de Valera and his *Irish Press* were concerned, Gallagher had two priceless qualities: total commitment to the cause and great journalistic flair.

However, as happens so frequently with editors and their proprietors, it was all to end in tears. In the bitterness of his departure he wrote to a former colleague: "In those four years you and I together made a great paper, courageous, strong and with a love and concern for the poor and the powerless...its influence was enormous because we had the news and we made the most of it." The conflict, he explained, arose out of the board's concern for finances and his concern lest the economies forced on him destroyed the paper's reputation for news-gathering. "...that clash uncovered another and deeper still one of personalities—though now an editorial matter. Out of that—it arose from a dismissal which to me was unjust—came my resignation."

To the board he had been more defiant. The *Irish Press*, he wrote in a memo, "was created by me out of the most mixed elements, trained, partly trained and untrained...men who for the most part were schooled in a journalism wholly foreign to the democratic and republican outlook which is the essential mark of this newspaper and on which its appeal to the people is based."

De Valera's initial anxiety that the capital available would fall short of what would see them through the launch and the initial build-up period proved only too justified. Stunned by the initial popular success of the paper, its competitors used every means at their disposal to frustrate it. Newsagents were encouraged not to stock it. The *Irish Independent* management objected to its being carried on the newspaper train and the board of the Great Southern Railway insisted that they hire a special train. De Valera appealed to the railways tribunal and got the decision reversed. The *Independent* took the matter to the High Court which reversed the railways tribunal's ruling.

An even bigger problem arose in regard to attracting advertising. De Valera's professed policy of supporting and encouraging home industry so as to provide a wider marketing base was, of course, *Irish Press* policy too. It was anathema to the British manufacturers who controlled most of the Irish market and whose advertising agents *Irish Press* representatives were sent to canvass. The young Erskine Childers, just down from Cambridge, was recruited as advertising manager and he had at least one unusual success. Having succeeded in getting an appointment with a senior executive of Dunlop the man brushed aside his spiel about the virtues of Mr de Valera's paper and asked: "Are you the same Childers as *The Riddle of the Sands*?" The young salesman admitted that his father had written the book, whereupon the Dunlop man started to quote verbatim from his favourite novel and immediately booked a series of advertisements.

Joe Walsh, who joined the paper in 1934 and edited it from 1962 until 1968, is under no illusions about the reasoning behind the lack of support. "The excuses as relayed to the paper's advertising representatives were many and varied but seldom true—the readers of that paper haven't got the purchasing power...it is only read by penniless rapparees...its policy is not in the best interests of the consumers. Yet it is clearly evident from a perusal of the national dailies of that period that these were not the real reasons. Large detergent advertisements, for example, appeared in *The Irish Times*, the readers of which were small in number and on the whole wealthy. No one believed that these readers did the family wash. It was seen as a form of subsidy. Finance and insurance institutions followed the soap companies lead. Solicitors, auctioneers and the smaller businesses, with similar prejudices, rubbed shoulders with them in this pro-British, snobbish attitude. It was a political attitude towards those who dared to question the treaty or to use the treaty to end our economic dependence on Britain..."

Penury soon became a fact of life at Burgh Quay. Frank Ridgeway, the cashier, would frequently have to empty the cash register at the front counter in order to pay an impatient creditor waiting in his office upstairs. And he often had to leave by the works entrance so as to avoid those demanding payment in the front office. He was the gentlest and the most civilised of men and these mild deceptions cannot have come easily to him. When I came to the *Press* he was company secretary and one of his tasks was to issue the vouchers with which air tickets were purchased. Unlike many cashiers who grow into believing that the funds they are issuing are from their own pockets, he never appeared to resent what to him must have often appeared as sheer profligacy.

With financial collapse likely, the US shareholders grew nervous and put in an American efficiency expert named Jack Harrington. There was immediate conflict. Poorly paid journalists resented the fact that despite the impecunious state of the company's finances, Harrington was billeted in the Gresham Hotel. He soon made his presence felt, involving himself in every department and, in Frank Gallagher's words, hiring an architect to reorganise the editorial room "to prevent the congregating of sports casuals and to eliminate the smell of drink."

This proved too much for the NUJ and an order went

out forbidding members to co-operate in any way with the hated Harrington.

Gallagher, who had welcomed Harrington and promised him full co-operation, used his influence with the staff to prevent this happening. Soon, however, the fiery American had turned the benign editor into his fiercest adversary. Gallagher was in his office when he heard a tirade of abuse coming from the newsroom and, on investigating, found Harrington publicly bawling out one of the editorial executives. In his official memo of complaint Gallagher noted that Harrington continued to berate the night editor in front of his subordinates "until vigorously checked by me."

This was too much for the fastidious and courteous editor, who immediately set about undermining him where it would likely have most effect—with de Valera himself. "Mr Harrington," he wrote to the Chief, "has the American view of workers—that they must be shown who is the boss and the way to show them is to sack somebody important...From my observations I am convinced that Mr Harrington knows nothing of conditions here and not so much about newspaper offices—Irish ones anyway—as he pretends." And to this he added a doleful plea about the current economies: "Last night we carried no picture of the Fr Griffin memorial because the art editor was afraid to bring the man back by car. There are times when a paper cannot afford to make a poor mouth."

De Valera, who probably had no other option, thought differently and on this occasion left his editor, confidant and friend hanging out to dry. The Frank Gallagher papers in the National Library contain three pathetic letters written to the Chief during this time. It appears that there were no replies. Gallagher never succeeded in grasping one of the most basic facts of newspaper publishing—that in a financial crisis the accountant will supersede even the most brilliant editor.

For a salary of £850 a year (£31,500 in 1992 money) Gallagher put in a gruelling six-day week which would astonish most of today's journalists. In his own meticulous way he worked out a work schedule headed: "Editor's duties as performed by Frank Gallagher."

His working day started at 11.30 am when he began to read and compare that morning's papers. Lunch was from 1 to 2; then he devoted an hour to reading English newspapers. There followed a ninety-minute break after which he left Sutton for the office. I suspect that this schedule was drawn up when he felt under threat from the board and the US "efficiency" expert. The schedule went on:

5 pm to 6 pm	See news editor, discuss contents, hear of that day's stories, read *Cork Examiner*.
7.15 to 7.30	Return to office.
7.30 to 8.00	Leader writers' conference.
8.15 to 8.30	General conference; all executives attend.
8.45 to 9.15	Callers interviewed.
9.15 to 10.00	Correspondence dealt with.
10.00 to 10.15	See financial editor and woman editor; check on sports misses and see sports editor.
10.15 to 10.30	Signing of important letters.
10.30 to 11.00	Cutline (break).

11.00 to 11.30	Deal with political copy and speeches requiring "policy heads."
11.30 to 12.00	Supervision of editorials.
12.00 to 1.30	The rush hour. Proofs gone through if possible; picture page passed; ticklish copy referred to editor dealt with; editorials revised in proof; lead discussed in conference with chief sub; short visit to store if required to push the paper through the last 15 minutes.
1.30 to 2.00	Rest and tag ends dealt with.
2.00—	Read Independent for "sticks" (exclusive stories or stories in which the opposition excels).

After that it was up on the bike and home to Sutton.

His departure from the *Irish Press* though rancorous didn't end his friendship with or his service to the chief. De Valera soon appointed him deputy director of Radio Éireann but on the outbreak of war moved him to his own department as head of the Government Information Bureau. Here, in the words of Maurice Gorham, "he became virtually chief censor, and in this capacity he was to impinge continually and irksomely on Radio Éireann." Soon he was also impinging irksomely on another strong-willed American, this time the notorious wartime US ambassador David Gray, who described him in a dispatch to Roosevelt as "the Irish Dr Goebbels," who was running de Valera's "propaganda machine...the most effective in the world now that Goebbels is dead." He wrote several books, including an account of his hunger-strikes as a Republican prisoner called *Days of Fear*. (John "Backbencher" Healy used to say that each of his successors was well equipped to write a sequel called *Nights of Fear*.)

Gallagher's energy was legendary. Everything was documented and the first sub-editors were given a set of instructions which incorporated themes which he addressed over and over in lengthy and pedantic correspondences with news agencies:

1: Always give the Irish angle in the headlines.

2: Do not use agency headlines: the other papers will have these.

3: Be on your guard against the habits of British and foreign news agencies who look at the world mainly through imperialist eyes. For instance:

(a) Do not pass the word "bandits" as a description of South American revolutionaries.

(b) Pirates and robbers in China are not necessarily communists and therefore should not be described as such.

(c) These agency stories show ignorance of Catholic practices and things: check all doubtful references in such copies.

(d) Propagandist attacks on Russia and other countries should not be served up as news.

(e) Do not make the *Irish Press* a Dublin paper—there are O'Connell Streets in other cities too.

And in what the historian Professor JJ Lee saw as "a residual Fianna Fáil aversion to the forces of law," Gallagher issued a further injunction that "it is not necessary to report every word of praise spoken to policemen" or to report judges' jokes "unless they are real jokes." "Should it be finally decided that we take your service," he wrote to the British manager of the powerful United Press Association, "I hope that we shall get some form of news of America other than is now supplied by agencies as a whole, namely an amalgam of gangster activities, divorces at Reno, Hollywood stories and prohibition raids. When one realises that America is a continent with intense political and cultural activity, it seems a shame that more is not heard of her nobler aspects."

He found time to write to the correspondent in Kilrush, Co Clare, querying the accuracy of her pig market reports. (She replied, indignantly, that in her ten years as a reporter the accuracy of her work had never been called into question.) He conducted a long and patient correspondence with another of his contributors, the feminist Hanna Sheehy Skeffington. Her association with the *Irish Press* ended acrimoniously with her accusing Gallagher of suppressing her (highly unfavourable) review of a new play by Lord Longford at the Gate. "In formally severing my connection with the *Irish Press* under its present editorial management," she wrote, "I wish to express my regret for a personal remark made by me at the end of our conversation last night. My only excuse was that I was provoked by the offensiveness of your attitude throughout, treating me, in fact, as if I were an illiterate. At the same time I recognise in cold blood that your lack of courtesy does not give me a similar licence."

Whatever his faults and failings, he played a huge part in the development of modern Irish journalism. Yet he is almost entirely forgotten. In more than twenty-five years I don't suppose I have heard his name mentioned more than half a dozen times in Burgh Quay, and I would be surprised if there are a dozen journalists under fifty in the country to whom his name means anything. Journalists tend to be honoured no more in death than in life, and while this in itself is no bad thing, I think it's a pity that Frank Gallagher's name doesn't live on in some scholarship or other award for the encouragement of young journalists. He was, after all, an enthusiast.

Many believed that the *Irish Press* wouldn't survive without him. They were wrong. Frank Gallagher's departure proved once again that even the most brilliant editors are expendable. The paper certainly lost some of its earlier panache but it struggled on until the Second World War (which it acknowledged only as "The Emergency") and which changed so many things, came to its rescue. As far as newspapers are concerned, the war was the greatest of levellers and it probably saved the *Irish Press* from extinction.

5

THE BEST OF TIMES

Then all at once the quarrel sank:
Everyone felt the same,
And every life became
A brilliant breaking of the bank,
A quite unlosable game.

Philip Larkin, "Annus Mirabilis"

On Wednesday, 22 January 1958, the Roman Catholic Archbishop of Dublin, the imperious Dr John Charles McQuaid, set out from his episcopal palace in Drumcondra to bless a vocational school recently erected in the south city suburb of Dundrum. Two of the three Dublin dailies sent reporters to cover the event. The *Irish Press* was represented by Maurice Liston, one of its senior and most colourful reporters. The *Irish Independent* sent John Healy, its aviation and diplomatic correspondent, then a junior recently arrived from the *Sligo Champion*. *The Irish Times*, still clearly identified as the Protestant paper, was not represented.

The archbishop was known to be impatient of newspapers and their representatives. His Lenten pastorals were submitted with the proviso that they be printed in full or not at all. His Grace disliked being photographed and some press photographers believed that his enthusiastic sprinkling of holy water in their direction as he blessed churches and other buildings was as much intended to blur their lenses as to bring them special graces. Only in the most exceptional circumstances would a reporter dare approach the Archbishop on public occasions. If the archbishop wanted publicity for his public utterances a script would be prepared in advance and handed to the waiting reporters by his chauffeur.

On this occasion the chauffeur had no script to offer so the two reporters—both expert shorthand writers—took a note of the Archbishop's public speech and typed it up while the reception was going on. Healy was anxious to get back to the office but Liston insisted that the report be shown to the Archbishop for vetting. Healy's protests were in vain. Liston, aware of the special relationship between the Archbishop and Major Vivion de Valera, was taking no chances.

As Dr McQuaid was about to leave, Maurice's bulky figure broke from the ranks of the attenders like the soothsayer in Caesar's triumphal procession. Having made his obeisance, he started to address the prelate in the booming, guttural tones which were a source of wonderment to all who heard them. He explained that as no script had been made available he and his colleague had taken a verbatim shorthand note and would His Grace be so kind as to look over what they had written so as to make sure he was happy with it?

His Grace took the foolscap page and, scanning it, appeared to be amused rather than annoyed. "Is this what I really said?" he asked with a grin. Much encouraged, Maurice assured him that it was indeed what he had said as his words had been taken down by two men with top-class shorthand. The archbishop then slowly folded the foolscap paper twice and tore it into neat quarters. Handing them back to the astonished Maurice he said: "If that was what I said, then I hadn't intended saying it." And after giving a final benediction to the little group, he disappeared in a flash of purple into his waiting car.

With a few honourable exceptions, the established reporters of that era were a docile lot, over-zealous in their desire to please the proprietor, the advertiser, the prelate and the politician. The era was characterised by an unhealthy willingness to accept the prepared statement, the prepared speech and the public-relations handout without demanding the opportunity of asking searching questions as well. Irish newspapers were largely a conduit through which government, church and commercial interests fed their messages and their ideas to the masses. The Sixties changed much of that.

Within five years of its arrival television had altered the face of Irish journalism. Irish print journalists suddenly found themselves in competition with a new breed of interviewer, people such as Brian Farrell and John O'Donoghue, who were often better educated, more confident and more professional than their colleagues in the newspapers. Above all, they were far less in awe of the people they were interviewing and far less inclined to be fobbed off with blandishments or prepared statements. The emphasis now was on the hard question demanding an immediate answer within the uncomfortable atmosphere of the TV studio. The age of the confrontational interview had arrived and, until they started to learn new tricks, the interviewees reeled with shock. To teach these tricks there sprang up what I sometimes described in Dubliner's Diary as "the sweet reasonableness industry"—schools of TV presentation where politicans and captains of industry learned how to kick to touch with inanities prefaced by "I'm glad you asked me that, Brian," and, most important of all, developed the technique of delivering pre-selected answers which often bore little or no relation to the questions.

By 1966 the *Evening Press*—still only twelve years old—had seen off the *Evening Mail* and was outselling the *Evening Herald*. The *Sunday Press* had achieved a circulation undreamt of by Irish standards and the biggest ever by an Irish Sunday newspaper. The *Irish Press*, though dipping, was still selling over 100,000 copies a day and under Tim Pat Coogan would soon be the subject of a resuscitation attempt. At *The Irish Times* Douglas Gageby and his news editor, Donal Foley, were transforming the established organ of Protestantism and unionism into a paper that would transcend the sectarian and political divide to become the leading daily journal of ideas and opinion.

These were the good times at Burgh Quay. We were, as Christy Mahon said in *The Playboy of the Western World*, "mounted on the springtide of the stars of luck." Luck, unfortunately, was too big a part of it for we were already freewheeling. There was more luck than analysis; more chance than planning. It was around this time that there crept into the terminology of Burgh Quay an insidious cliché that became the stock answer to practically every attempt at innovation. Some changes were made—chiefly in the daily paper—but they were not enough, and they were not sustained. Those who tried to innovate were frequently greeted with the phrase which nearly became our epitaph: "You do not change a winning formula."

In 1966 I was too junior and too inexperienced to have been aware of the warning signs. One man who did see them was Conor O'Brien, then editor of the *Evening Press*. Of all the editors I have worked with, Conor O'Brien was the most impressive. In those days he displayed all the attributes of the great editor: he had guts, brains and a sense of decency and fair play. He also appeared to have been particularly fortunate when nature's gifts were being distributed. He was handsome, witty and gregarious, and he had an easy and relaxed manner with his subordinates.

He had taken over at the *Evening Press* from Douglas Gageby, who had departed on his mission to revolutionise *The Irish Times*. Gageby and Vivion de Valera had been fellow officers in the army during "The Emergency" and they had become friends. Between them they gave the *Evening Press* its identity and saw it through the difficult early years. By the late 1960s Conor had ideas for hardening up the paper and making it more responsive to the demands of the age. He wanted to feature hard exposé-type stories and in this area he particularly wanted to investigate the running of the Irish Hospitals' Sweepstakes. Much of this was anathema to Major de Valera, who, already hooked on "you do not change a winning formula," resisted change.

There were other difficulties. O'Brien had floated the idea that one of the three editors should be on the board of the company—a suggestion that was as appealing to Major de Valera as a proposal for an outing to the Folies Bergères might be to a Carthusian novice-master. Conor was also aware of the problems that active membership of the NUJ posed for editorial executives and favoured a separate organisation for them. This idea didn't find favour either. Conor finally had to make up his mind to leave Burgh Quay when he was offered the editorship of the *Sunday Independent.*

The relationship between a newspaper proprietor and his editor can be a difficult one even when—as sometimes happens—the editor is a natural sycophant. Editors who wish to maintain even a modicum of independence must normally be prepared to walk a tightrope. Proprietors such as the late Lord Thompson of Fleet who never interfered in editorial matters are rare. Many—Northcliffe, Beaverbrook and Hearst being prime examples—are natural bullies who become thoroughly corrupted by power. Others—Rupert Murdoch is a contemporary example—are feverish empire-builders who condone abysmal editorial standards for the sake of profit. Virtually all newspaper proprietors are solid establishment figures with a vested interest in preserving the status quo and fostering the interests of the establishment. Many editors live in fear of the proprietor and devote too much of their creative energy to placating him. Conor O'Brien was an impatient man and, I believe, he tried to push the management too fast; he was impatient of the Republican and religious ethos of Burgh Quay. This sometimes led to petty restrictions. During the 1961 visit of Princess Margaret and her husband, Anthony Armstrong-Jones, one of the *Press* photographers asked Armstrong-Jones, himself a photographer, to take his camera and shoot a picture of his wife. He obliged but it was felt that to use the picture would be kowtowing to British royalty.

Conor O'Brien was fortunate in that he had about him some highly talented department heads in whom he could have the fullest confidence. Tim Pat Coogan was his deputy, and a more confident, self-assured deputy it would be hard to find. Many deputy editors see the role as that of a caretaker—someone who takes over when the boss is away and even then acts as if he were still on the premises. That wasn't Tim Pat's style. He had been made an executive at a remarkably young age. He was ambitious and often impetuous. His headlines tended to be colourful and when the Soviets put the first man in space he excelled himself with a banner headline across the front page which said: "Red Male In The Sunrise."

Conor's features editor, Sean McCann, combined a flair for layout with the ability to cajole the best writers in the country into contributing to the paper. Sean O'Faolain, Benedict Kiely, Kate O'Brien, Frank O'Connor—all fell in with Sean's ideas and gladly produced articles for him. He also had the common touch and a sense of timing which gave him an instinct for what was currently absorbing the readers' interests. Sean was a most civilised colleague and I worked happily with him as a feature writer and later as his deputy. When he reached sixty he retired to enjoy and write about his twin hobbies, wine and roses.

Sean Ward, who took over as editor of the *Evening Press* when Conor left, had been news editor of that paper and later chief news editor of the Press group. His father, Terry Ward, had joined the paper as a reporter in the Thirties and spent most of his career in Fleet Street as London editor of the *Irish Press*.

Unlike most editors, Sean hadn't come up through the sub-editing department and he knew practically nothing about newspaper layout and design. To the dismay of the news staff he decided that he would delegate most of his responsibilities in this area and concentrate on what he knew best—news, sport and administration. That resulted in tough times for both the news and sports editors, for Ward was always a hard taskmaster. Conor O'Brien was a hard act to follow; yet it was Sean Ward who succeeded in bringing the sales of the paper to their highest-ever peak.

Apart from his news-gathering skills, the qualities he brought to the editorship were a strong sense of decency and fair play, excellent administrative ability (something of a rarity in editors), tenacity and hard work. He kept a low public profile and was at his desk every morning before eight. All the members of his staff knew that as long as he was there they were never likely to suffer from a swelled head. But they could also be certain that they were not going to be stabbed in the back. And that, in the newspaper world, is often a luxury.

Sean Ward has another quality which is by no means universal among editors. He has always kept a tight rein on his personal views and prejudices and does not allow them to interfere with his journalism. During my Dubliner's Diary years he has allowed me considerable freedom of expression. Con Houlihan, I know, has had the same experience.

Recruiting that same Mr Houlihan was one of Ward's major contributions to the *Evening Press*. Con has become something of a legend and, as far as the paper is concerned, a big commercial asset. Recruiting him wasn't difficult— the two men met in the Silver Swan—and Ward reckoned quite rightly that if Houlihan could write about sport as he talked about it the result should be interesting. The difficulty lay in keeping him.

Con is a prima donna. Like all performers, he loves adulation. And I suspect that he is heir to a fine legacy of the doubts and insecurities that bedevil even the most brilliant and most successful writers. From the very beginning he was a huge success and within a short time he had the statutory retinue of fans, genuine *aficionados* and hangers-on. The public image has been as carefully cultivated as that of Bernard Shaw. His costume is simple and serviceable—the anorak being *de rigueur* even when working in tropical conditions. Irish sports journalists have (with some justification) been described as "fans with typewriters." Con has no typewriter—he has consistently refused to recognise the invention. His copy is handwritten, a single paragraph to the page.

As with all celebrities, there is a gulf between the public and private person. Con's public image is of a wild, dishevelled and highly disorganised man. Dishevelled he sometimes may be—wild and disorganised he certainly is not. Few journalists are as disciplined or as single-minded as Con. Unlike most newspaper journalists he corrects his own proofs, working meticulously through the computer print-outs and threatening resignation if the slightest corrections are not immediately attended to. His prose can be as spare as Hemingway's and like all great professionals, he makes the finished product look simple and effortless.

He has made an enormous contribution to the *Evening Press*—and not only in terms of attracting and holding on to readers. Like his hero William Hazlitt, he is the common man blessed with extraordinary powers of perception and expression. His wide learning and love of literature have rubbed off on many a colleague. Like many of those who are "come of Kerry clay and rock" there is a roughish side to him. In the early days he was prone to tantrums, particularly around the time his contract came up for renewal. On those occasions he would insist that the call to the bog or to the potato field was too strong to resist. At the oddest of hours he would phone the editor at home and announce that he was on his way to Castle Island and that he wouldn't be back. Fortunately for the *Evening Press* and for all of us who work there, Con hasn't carried out his threat.

Con came to us during that lull before the start of the Northern Ireland upheaval—a difficult time for newspapers for the simple reason that very little was happening. In those days the Dublin evening papers tended to be very parochial, carrying in their early country editions yards of cheap copy chronicling the misdemeanours of nonentities culled from the proceedings of the district courts of the country.

It makes good commercial sense for a newspaper to regard its own circulation area as the centre of the universe. But in those days the notion was carried too far. Everything had to be localised. An earthquake in Brazil in which thousands had perished might well bear the banner headline "Irish Nun's Miracle Escape in Quake Horror."

Foreign news agency reports were scoured for a possible Irish angle. I once followed up a UPI paragraph about a gang slaying in Chicago in which one of the dead was named as Michael Collins. "We were wondering," I asked the detective in charge of the case, "if Michael Collins happened to be Irish?" The cop was most encouraging. "He may well be Irish," he drawled, "but he's as black as the ace of spades."

It would be several years before there was any real attempt to come to grips with our provincialism. We took most of our ideas from London, scouring the Fleet Street papers not only for follow-ups but also for feature ideas. Over the years I became increasingly impatient at this penchant of ours to look to London as if it were the centre of the universe. To an extent we still do it. That is why we slavishly regurgitate even the most hysterical anti-Irish ravings of hack journalists working on the most discredited gutter newspapers.

Yet when a big story did break we were always more than able to cope with it, taking as our motto Oscar Wilde's dictum that "nothing succeeds like excess." From its inception the *Press* established a reputation as a superb news-gathering machine.

When I arrived most of the amateurs had gone and the emphasis was on recruiting bright, hungry young men and women who might, as they say in the racing business, be expected to train on. The system worked well enough, but— except for a few years during the Seventies—there was always a high turnover of staff. Many left because the management wouldn't match the few extra shillings they had been offered elsewhere; others went because they felt their ambitions couldn't be realised under the Burgh Quay regime.

But we had fun. As long as one had the entrance fee (in those days it was generally computed as half a crown) to the Silver Swan, Mulligan's or the Scotch House, one could be sure of genial and rumbustious companionship.

Of all the colleagues of those days who slipped in and out of those worthy pubs, Sean Lynch was probably the most remarkable. Tall, handsome, and always immaculately turned out, he was an impressive figure. He was a splendid hard-news reporter: accurate, confident, quick to assimilate facts and nobody's fool—the kind of reporter every news editor likes to have around him when a big story breaks.

But side by side with all these qualities there existed a Walter Mitty element which his friends took for granted but which astounded those who knew him only casually. Sean had an imagination which frequently transported him into the most exotic surroundings and involved him in the most fantastic situations.

Once he opened the typewriter this side of his personality ceased to exist and he became the dispassionate, highly accurate reporter. But in the Silver Swan he flew military jets, performed emergency neurosurgery, disarmed

Sicilian bandits and rescued drowning beauties from shark-infested seas. This propensity for tall tales led to his being called "the lip"—a soubriquet that was much to his liking.

Sean left journalism early to become public-relations adviser to Dermot Ryan, an entrepreneur with newly acquired political ambitions. Careerwise it was a disastrous move. For all his imaginative abilities, Sean was at heart a very straightforward and uncomplicated man and poorly equipped to deal with the internal company politics that engulf every powerful chief executive. He was deeply unhappy and soon returned to Burgh Quay. But out of misfortune came good. Sean fell in love with Gillian Wymes, Ryan's private secretary, and soon we were attending their wedding in Greystones.

Their happiness together was to be brief for Sean was the first of our young group in Burgh Quay who would "fear no more the heat o' the sun." He contracted Hodgkin's disease, which has claimed the lives of many young men of talent, among them JM Synge.

The confident immortality of youth was crumbling. Sean's death was a devastating blow to Gillian, their young son and his family. For me it was not alone the loss of a good friend but the first real reminder of my own mortality. I had been with Sean a few hours before he died and later with our friend Michael Keane I helped to make his funeral arrangements. Then in the early hours I had to return to Burgh Quay to write Dubliner's Diary.

For a journalist the luxury known as writer's block is not only unaffordable but regarded as somewhat shameful and unprofessional. The professional always produces—the amateur talks about producing. That night not even one inane and cliché-ridden phrase would come. The dawn began to break over the Liffey and I started to feel slight panic. "Come on, Lip," I said audibly. "You mustn't let this happen to me." My prayer was answered and I polished off the 1,500 words without difficulty.

The habitués of the Swan were scattering. Sean Kennedy sold it to a man called Butterly. "All's changed, changed Butterly," cried a disconsolate Des Twomey after being told by the new manager that the credit facilities provided by the previous proprietor had now been rescinded.

Soon the Swan would close for good to become yet another derelict site, another blotch on the once fair face of Dublin. Some of the older regulars were dying off too— Gerry Leacy, a talented sub-editor and dedicated Gordon's-and-Schweppes man, who on becoming PRO for Watney's Red Barrell was condemned to drink a brew which in his cups he would vilify with all the passion of a Free Presbyterian condemning papism, died of a heart attack in Bristol; Bobby Johnson, the gregarious and kind-hearted music critic who conducted a running battle with the managing editor in an effort to get his fee increased from the miserly thirty shillings per notice, also made a sudden exit. (After one of several resignations over fees Bobby's parting shot to WJR was: "You may get a better music critic, Bill, but I'm damned if you'll ever get a cheaper one"). The urbane and cultured Des Twomey departed (as did Maureen Browne) to the *Irish Medical Times*; Conor O'Brien had already gone to Middle Abbey Street and, in keeping with the apartheid system which somehow seems to govern newspaper pubs, now confined his drinking to the Oval across the river.

In the carefree days when I first came to Dublin I shared a flat in Rathgar Road with two Sligo colleagues, Pat Chatten and Paddy Clancy, and a third Sligo man, John Hooks, who though not in journalism knew more about it than many who were. The flat was to become a sort of club-cum-embassy for Sligo people with many refugees arriving. We were a raucous lot, but John (Hooxi to his friends) exercised a quiet authority over us. Slight of frame, big of heart and blessed with the rare gift of contentment, Hooxi was a thoroughly good man and until his early death in 1990 remained one of my closest friends.

During our occupancy of the flat he married the *Irish Press* editorial secretary, Betty O'Driscoll (known to all in Burgh Quay as Miss Betty) and suddenly life at No 82 became infinitely more civilised. Before this it could be stark, the culinary arrangements frequently hampered by our inevitable mid-week penury. Miss Betty put manners on all of us.

Soon the Rathgar Road homestead would break up too. Paddy Clancy and Pat Chatten left for London to get more experience. John and Miss Betty set up their home on the foothills of the Dublin mountains. On 30 September, 1968 I covered the roll-out of the first Boeing 747 in Seattle—my last assignment as a bachelor. Five days later Maureen and I were married in her home parish of Bruff.

6

ALL CHANGE HERE

> Oh ye hypocrites, ye can discern the face of the sky: but
> can ye discern the signs of the times?
>
> Matthew: 16: 3

Discerning the signs of the times is what successful newspaper management is all about. And this is not, as St Matthew was at pains to point out, a trick that is easily performed.

Newspaper proprietors and editors—whose fortunes or necks depend on it—frequently do the most lunatic things in their efforts to keep in touch with the street. Lord Northcliffe used to give lifts to all and sundry, and at Northcliffe House many an executive head rolled because of a judgement on the *Daily Mail* handed down by some tramp or rustic in the back seat of his lordship's Rolls Royce.

Today's newspaper proprietors are more likely to pay large sums to some market research company rather than give lifts in their Rolls Royces. But the quest is the same, and sometimes the results may be no more enlightening. St Matthew's trenchant words, meanwhile, still mock us.

The Sixties saw the breaking up of the old order in Irish journalism, the arrival of the RTE television service in 1961 being the chief catalyst. I often wonder if the other power brokers of the land, the politicians, the prelates, the union bosses and the money men, shared President de Valera's sense of foreboding as the cameras were switched on to show the snow falling on Dublin that New Year's Eve?

Did the politicians realise that the age of their butter-box rhetoric was over? Did the bishops of Ireland, viewing in their isolated episcopal palaces throughout the country, realise that the age in which they could send their pastoral letters to the newspapers with the proviso that they be printed in full or not at all were gone for ever? How many of the newspaper proprietors realised that their fear about the deflection of advertising revenue to the new medium was but a part of their problem and that their comfortable cartel would soon be rocked to its foundations.

Were they all as fretful as the President? "...I feel somewhat afraid...Never before was there in the hands of man an instrument so powerful to influence the thoughts and actions of the multitude..." And what did the President's eldest son, Major Vivion de Valera, controlling director and editor-in-chief of *Irish Press* Newspapers, think as he contemplated this winter scene while his father looked into his own heart and did not like a bit of what he found there?

Major de Valera was then at the height of his powers as a newspaper proprietor. Along with his general manager, Jack Dempsey, he had recently been responsible for the publishing success of the decade—the founding of the *Evening Press*. Doubts had been raised then about the success of this venture especially since there had been a previous abortive attempt at starting an evening paper in Burgh Quay.

In 1954 he gave the final say to his father. There had been long and inconclusive discussions by the board. Father and son sat down one evening in Eamon de Valera's house in Booterstown Avenue and even though they discussed every aspect of the proposal they couldn't come to a conclusion either. Then as the old man was going up the stairs to bed he turned and said: "In the end, it is nearly always better to do something."

Vivion de Valera was well able to discern the signs of the times then, and when the new decade arrived he had not lost his touch. To start with, he realised that there would have to be a new approach to political coverage. This was a real problem because the bulk of the Fianna Fáil party, let alone the *Irish Press* shareholders, still looked on the *Irish Press* as the Fianna Fáil house magazine.

At the start of the Sixties the umbilical cord that joined the *Irish Press* to Fianna Fáil was still intact and there was constant pressure on Major de Valera to increase the paper's commitment to the party. The bald statement in the first leading article that "we are not the organ of an individual, of a group, or a party" was, like all holy writ, subject to much casuistry. But when all the nods and winks had stopped, the popular perception of the *Irish Press* was that it was the kept newspaper of Fianna Fáil. But the party had to look to the controlling director for its favours and the controlling director could, and sometimes did, issue a rebuff. There were many—and there still are many—in Fianna Fáil who believe that Major de Valera did the party no favours at all when, in 1963, he made Michael Mills political correspondent of the *Irish Press*.

At the time the appointment can scarcely have caused many ripples. Mills had impeccable credentials. A skilled reporter who had come to journalism after testing a vocation to the religious life with the Passionists, he was politically active and had been secretary of a Fianna Fáil cumann. The worst fears any party stalwart might be expected to have at the time was that Mills was reputed to be a bit of an intellectual. They could hardly imagine that within two decades this civilised and courageous man would become one of the great hate figures of a large section of the party and that the relentless antipathy of some of the party's leading figures would pursue him even after he had left journalism to become Ireland's first ombudsman.

In the Burgh Quay that I knew in the Sixties, Michael Mills was the leader of a group of journalists whose *gravitas* and hard work balanced out the bohemianism and the fecklessness of several others. These serious people included the three editors and most of the editorial executives as well as a troupe of reporters and sub-editors who, day after day and night after night, ensured that the papers came out. Vivion de Valera knew that with the advent of television the days of reverential political coverage were over. He knew too that adjusting to this would, as far as the *Irish Press* was concerned, be a difficult and even dangerous process. After selecting Mills for the trapeze he told him: "Tell the truth and be fair, and provided you comply with these two requirements I'll stand over what you do."

Michael Mills was appearing on a TV programme the first time I saw him. It was during my *Limerick Leader* days and I was having a pint with Pat Finn in Willie Gleeson's. Practically all the customers were watching what must have been one of the first productions of the political programme *The Hurler on the Ditch* on which Mills was a regular panellist. That evening some particularly contentious matter was being discussed and Mills delivered a reasoned but quite acerbic response which was highly critical of Fianna Fáil. The landlord, a solid and kindly vintner who was decidedly not of the Fianna Fáil persuasion, gazed in wonder and amazement at the flickering black-and-white screen perched precariously and at some altitude over the snug. As Mills finished his piece, Willie wiped his hands on his shop coat and, as was his custom, addressed his clientèle succinctly but *en masse*. "I presume, gentlemen," he said, "that your man has another job lined up that he can go to in the morning." The publican's reaction was not untypical. Having resigned from Fianna Fáil, Mills demonstrated an independence of mind which amazed the public, delighted most of his colleagues and confounded and dismayed a sizeable section of Fianna Fáil. Yet in spite of many strains the experiment worked and within a few years Michael Mills had become probably the most respected political correspondent of the day.

My own view is that his contribution to Irish journalism in general and to the *Irish Press* in particular is a considerable one. As far as the *Irish Press* was concerned he played a pivotal role in earning a new-found respect for the paper in a constituency which was becoming more and more independent politically and less and less willing to absorb propaganda masquerading as journalism. That, I think, would be the view of most journalists of the period. But it is by no means universal. The escalation of the Northern troubles and the political upheavals of the 1970s created fierce tensions in Burgh Quay.

The decision to adopt a strong Republican line throughout the Seventies and into the Eighties was ideological and in keeping with the sincerely held views of Major de Valera and his editor, Tim Pat Coogan. But there was much dissension among the readership. On a visit home to Hospital in the mid-Seventies I got a shock to find that my brother no longer bought the *Irish Press*, thus breaking a family link that went back to the foundation of the paper.

The dichotomy between what Major Vivion de Valera TD was saying in Leinster House and what Major Vivion de Valera, editor-in-chief, was saying in Burgh Quay was a source of wonder to many. The late John Healy—an old Burgh Quay hand himself—tackled this issue in his Backbencher column in *The Irish Times*.

The Major, Healy declared, was "two divine persons" in regard to the Provos. "He has been careful to keep his roles separate and sentiments of understanding of the Provos which appear in his paper have never been repeated in the house," Healy wrote in March 1974. "In the house his concern repeatedly has been for the dignity of the house and its relevance to our society. He has made many fine speeches on this theme. His paper's tacit concern for the Provos has often been attributed to Tim Pat Coogan, the current editor, but old Burgh Quay hands think that in political matters it is de Valera's policy that is printed."

Nine months earlier Healy was drawing attention to the paper's treatment of Jack Lynch. "The party's official journal, the *Irish Press*," he wrote, "is running a lovely anti-Lynch line and you will find many takers in the party for the suggestion that Burgh Quay has now come out much more in the open in savaging Lynch's dove policy. It is true you'll find Jack's picture in the paper now and again. You'll even find his speeches. But don't look for Jack's words of placatory wisdom in the editorial section. On the contrary..."

During the winter of 1980 there occurred an incident which bordered on a palace revolution. Seven Republican prisoners had been on hunger-strike in the H-blocks ostensibly for the right to wear their own clothes. By November passions were running high and as always on these occasions, great tension had been generated by the prospect of the carnage and violence that frequently occurs in the wake of hunger-strikes.

Early that November Gerry Fitt made a speech in the House of Commons in which he urged the government not to grant political status to the hunger-strikers. Fitt reasoned that granting it would escalate rather than diminish the violence by enhancing recruitment to the Provisional IRA. He cited the 1972 situation when he had been in favour of granting political status in the hope that it would diminish the violence but the almost immediate result was savage bombing campaigns in Belfast, Coleraine and Claudy. He also said that most Irish Protestants— particularly those in the North—regarded Cardinal Ó Fiaich as someone who gave some sort of tacit support to the objectives of the IRA.

On 12 November the *Irish Press* responded with a leading article to this and Fitt's subsequent appearance on RTE's *Today Tonight*. The leader accused Fitt of attacking his own people and of "trampling on the emotions which he must know from first-hand knowledge of West Belfast are rising daily and hourly in his native place." It threw in a grudging tribute to Fitt "for bearing the heat and burden of the day for many years in Belfast" but regretted that he was now succumbing to "the old disease of the Irish at Westminster, 'the tone of the house,' that siren call of English manners and English interests that has seduced so many Irish representatives away from their allegiances and those of the people who returned them in the first place..." This was fairly routine stuff. What caused the furore was the opening paragraph, which read: "Poor Gerry Fitt! The old jibe that whenever the British theatre required a stage Irishman, there was always an Irishman found to play the part has acquired a new vitality."

By this time the journalistic staff was polarised in regard to the North and many regarded the leading article as the last straw. In normal circumstances disagreement with the line taken in a leading article would cause no more ripples than a few wry or cynical jokes in the newsroom or around the subs table. But these were not normal circumstances, least of all for journalists. They were harrowing, divisive and dangerous times. Journalists were often the subject of threats. (When I worked on the newsdesk I got a phone call one morning from an anonymous paramilitary who told me he wanted a certain event covered, adding the rider: "And if it isn't, Mr O'Toole, we won't have any bother finding out what schools your children go to.") Yet in Dublin we were given but a taste of the vicious intimidation that has permanently enslaved thousands in Northern Ireland.

In those days it took some courage to refuse to put something in the collection box when the Provos came to collect in the pubs and it took very real courage to denounce them in print. The names of three courageous writers stand out: in *Hibernia*, Hugh Leonard baited and enraged the Provos on an almost weekly basis with his withering contumely; in the *Evening Press* Con Houlihan consistently criticised their philosophies and methods, and the *Irish Independent* columnist Desmond Rushe was also trenchant in his condemnation. Nowadays it is fashionable and easy to condemn the Provos—back in the Seventies it could be dangerous.

Gerry Fitt was admired and liked by many journalists and even those who hadn't worked in the North and didn't know him personally could hardly have been unaware of his courage. Many of us felt that the opening paragraph of the leader exceeded the bounds of fair comment and thirty-one journalists put their names to a telegram dissociating themselves from it. Fitt was moved by the gesture and he told *The Irish Times* that he was "grateful and humbled by it."

Tim Pat Coogan is remembered as an editor principally for his consuming concern for the Northern troubles and this has, I think, obscured his other achievements as a journalist and as an editor. I have worked closely with about a dozen editors and all of them possessed in varying degrees what sportsmen call "the killer instinct." All but one were deeply ambitious for the editorial chair, and some were thoroughly ruthless in achieving and even more so in holding on to it. William Hazlitt wrote that "it is utterly impossible to persuade an Editor that he is nobody" and it is true enough that many newspaper editors are aggressive and intolerant. It isn't hard to see why. They shoulder great responsibilities, often have to take the rap for the faults of their subordinates and are generally more easily toppled than any other journalist on the paper.

Tim certainly had the killer instinct. As an editor he was a very tough nut indeed. He was capable of ruthlessness, yet he helped more lame dogs over stiles than any editor I have known. He could be generous and magnanimous, and he could devastate a subordinate with a single withering put-down. His principal strength was that he had great guts—he was always a strong editor in an age when strong editors are becoming an increasingly rare breed.

Ultimately, when the paper was about to take a direction which was out of joint with most of what he believed in and stood for, he had the guts to get out. Resignation on a point of principle is old hat in journalism nowadays; most editors and executives have been tamed into meekly surrendering much of their editorial authority to the marketing gurus and the accountants. It is hard to blame them. Editors are hired hands like everyone else in the paper and they have mortgages to pay and children to educate. Resignation is the litmus test of guts in an editor.

In most matters Tim was very much in tune with the age and he was an innovator. He loved all aspects of politics and he delighted in being in a position to influence affairs. Shortly after I joined the *Press* he sent me to interview Archbishop John Charles McQuaid on his return from an *ad limina* and specifically instructed me to ask if he had offered his resignation to the Pope.

Junior as I was, I knew this was treacherous territory. News-gathering techniques were changing, I knew, but they hadn't changed to the point where one could readily doorstep John Charles McQuaid, Archbishop of Dublin and Primate of Ireland, and quiz him on a matter which was known to be of extreme sensitivity. Besides, the archbishop has a very special relationship with the de Valera family. The major had been his pupil at Blackrock College. They had interests in common—astronomy and target-shooting. When the major's young brother was killed in a riding accident the then Fr McQuaid spent many hours consoling his mother. The friendship between the major's father and the archbishop had cooled because of Dr McQuaid's role in the rumpus over the Health Act of 1953, and the major had also fallen out with him over a matter of protocol in the Pro-Cathedral. But this row, I felt, only made my mission of insolence more hazardous.

As I had time to spare before the encounter I went down to the Silver Swan. Terry O'Sullivan and Conor

O'Brien were there and I told them what Tim Pat was up to. "Poor you," said Conor. "Poor you, indeed," said Terry O. "It won't surprise me if he turns you into a toad."

At the airport I was dismayed to find no other reporters awaiting the archbishop. Osmond Dowling, his newly appointed press officer, was standing guard in the VIP room, sending up great clouds of smoke from what must have been the most overworked pipe in Ireland.

The archbishop eventually sailed in on what appeared to be a cloud of purple. There was much ring-kissing and reverencing. Ossie Dowling, unaware of my vile intent, introduced us. I got down on my right knee and kissed the archbishop's ring. He looked at me intently and quizzically. My mouth was dry. I felt clammy and slightly dizzy.

It was time to strike. "Your Grace," I ventured, "we understand there are rumours that you may have tendered your resignation to the Holy Father."

The archbishop's head jerked backwards as if an electric shock had come rushing up his spine. I thought I heard a faint strangulated gasp from where Ossie Dowling stood. The archbishop's steely eyes started to frost over. An eternity passed.

When the archbishop eventually spoke, his voice was a controlled whisper.

"Who did you say you were?"

I told him.

"Who sent you?"

I told him.

"And who, pray, informed Mr Coogan of these rumours?"

I said I didn't know.

There was a long pause. The archbishop sat down but gave no indication that I should do the same. "Take a statement," he said.

With his slender hands crossed across his lap, Dr McQuaid now looked perfectly relaxed as he dictated easily and precisely. "The Archbishop of Dublin," he began, "the Most Reverend JC McQuaid DD, had a meeting with the Holy Father at Castel Gandolfo—two words, spelt C-a-s-t-e-l G-a-n-d-o-l-f-o—full stop. The archbishop conveyed to the Holy Father the filial devotion...of the faithful people of Ireland...full stop...in response the Holy Father...imparted to the faithful people of Ireland...his paternal apostolic benediction...full stop." My question had been ignored. And now the hand with the indulgenced ring was put forward again and I made obeisance for the second time. Ossie Dowling, looking like the wedding guest after his encounter with the ancient mariner, led me out.

While I have always disagreed with Tim Pat's political views, we have always had a most cordial working relationship and when I wanted to go to Trinity College late in life Tim most generously helped smooth my path. I was delighted that his first book on becoming a full-time author—the Michael Collins biography—was such a big commercial success.

In the early days of his editorship Tim Pat gathered around him a number of bright and often controversial people including David Marcus, literary editor, TP O'Mahony, Mary Kenny, John Boland, later to become features editor of the *Evening Press*, and Vincent Browne, who went on to edit the *Sunday Tribune*. Tom O'Mahony and I became good friends. I was covering aviation then and Tom used to claim that, as religious affairs correspondent, his jurisdiction began where mine ended—the edge of the troposphere, roughly 35,000 feet above the earth. Tom's robust style of questioning coupled with his liberal views caused the starch to wilt in many a wimple and mitre. And if being a liberal wasn't enough, as a sideline he writes spicy novels with titles such as *Sex and Sanctity* and *The Taoiseach's Mistress*.

After *Sex and Sanctity* came out the major had Tom in for one of his philosophical chats. As with everyone else who was subject to these, Tom knew that the real message was likely to come as a coda. On the major's desk was a copy of *Sex and Sanctity* with its Robert Ballagh cover showing a pair of frilly panties and a clerical collar draped over a chair. Nothing was said about the book for ages. Eventually the major picked up the book and started to contemplate the cover. He had, he said, no wish whatever to interfere with Tom's freedom to engage in literary endeavours. That was his own affair entirely. He would only ask him to consider the impact of this kind of artistic expression on the more sensitive members of the senior clergy. He wasn't, he explained, particularly worried about "our side of the house" (the major's metaphor for the Roman Catholic church) but those on "the other side of the house" were more easily scandalised by these things. The Roman Catholic clergy, he felt, were better able to take things like this in their stride.

Tom thanked the major for his concern and assured

him that he would think carefully about what he had said. The session had no long-term success but the major was in his grave by the time *The Taoiseach's Mistress* came out with its lurid cover and its spectacular and highly publicised launch by Ms Christine Keeler. Tom O'Mahony wrote seriously and well on religious affairs for the *Irish Press* and, despite the novels, gained the respect of several senior clerics. Alas, he left the paper in the first wave of redundancies and found a true spiritual home in "de paper" (the *Cork Examiner*), where he continues to illuminate matters theological and sensual.

Although my own career was to take me through several departments and included sub-editing, news-editing and feature-writing, I have always regarded myself first and foremost as a reporter. Scarred and scared after my *Limerick Leader* experience, it was very heaven to be part of a very fine news team where despite the lunacies and the roistering there was a high degree of professionalism as well as camaraderie and sheer good fun. The regime in Burgh Quay may have been tough but there were many compensations.

And as if to make up for my misfortunes in Limerick, I had a long run of good luck just after my arrival. Dispatched to Mayo in search of *Sunday Press* "specials" (soft, often slightly inflated stories, usually with an off-beat angle and preferably of eccentric content ranging from five-legged calves to cures for baldness) photographer Tom McElroy and I chanced upon a long-forgotten killing that was very sensational at the time. We knocked on every door in the village and flooded the *Evening Press* with exclusive coverage.

Just as that story ended, another big tragedy involving a car going over a quay wall occurred a few miles away. Then with Eddie McDonnell I chanced upon an eccentric Scottish poet who had eloped with a peer's daughter and was being hunted by his enraged lordship who was intent on horsewhipping him. After that superbly illustrated story I noticed to my great satisfaction that some of my senior colleagues, men who had seen it all and in the Silver Swan would write off an earthquake as a hiccup, were treating me with new-found respect. Conor O'Brien came in to the newsroom and congratulated me. (Years later I discovered he had sought a bonus for me and the photographer but management refused on the grounds that it would set a precedent.)

The decision didn't surprise me. At that time it was company policy to restrict even by-lines for reporters lest they got notions and increased their market value elsewhere. Alas, in my case even this prudence failed to prevent the onset of an attack of cockiness and delusions of professional grandeur quite out of keeping with either my worth or my position. Unlike my cuter colleagues I was at that time not very good at interpreting the nuances and subtleties of Burgh Quay. I was full of enthusiasm and, I like to think, quite a good young reporter but I was a hopeless office politician.

Then for reasons that seemed perfectly good at the time I resigned. As air correspondent I had been invited to Seattle to cover the biggest aviation story of the decade—the first flight of a Boeing 747. I had already been there for the roll-out, but this was the real thing. Aviation correspondents were going from all over the world and the Boeing company was paying all expenses. In its wisdom the management decided to send one of the executives who also used the trip to visit a sick uncle in California.

This wasn't the only reason for my departure but I defected to Hugh MacLoughlin's Creation Group, where I became managing editor of Ireland's first free sheet newspaper, *The Dublin Post*, and where I was paid the then enormous salary of £100 a week.

Creation was a magazine house, quite different to newspapers, and while I found Mr MacLoughlin a novel and stimulating proprietor I soon realised that matters were not going to work out.

I limped back to Burgh Quay. After letting me hang out to dry for a respectable interval WJR told me I could have my job back. On the day of my interview he left me standing in the corridor outside his door feeling chastened and embarrassed as my former colleagues passed up and down.

After what seemed to me an eternity the pictures editor, Liam Flynn, who had built up the finest team of award-winning photographers in the country, came down the corridor and asked what the hell I was doing standing there. Liam was furious. He threw open WJR's door, ordered me inside and amazed me, WJR and probably himself by announcing to the great man that this wasn't good enough.

In the circumstances it was one of the kindest acts I have ever experienced.

7

DUBLINER'S DIARY: THE UNKIND WORD

Give me a hint, dear sir, a taste merely, of that stream of
calumny, which, according to the Bishop of Meath, rolls
down the streets of our favourite towns, taking a little
fresh venom at every house it passes.

Mrs Piozzi: letter to an unnamed friend, quoted in *A History
of the Diocese of Meath by J. Healy*

Dubliner's Diary lies towards the heart of the *Evening Press*
and is in some ways the voice of the paper. Thanks to its
first full-time incumbent, the late Terry O'Sullivan, it played
a sizeable role in the paper's early success. The day I took
over Dubliner's Diary Major Vivion de Valera summoned
me to the boardroom for one of his chats. Staff members
who found themselves subject to these impromptu sessions
suspected that the major's real purpose was to keep people
alert. His main point would usually emerge obliquely. This
kept people on their toes for it was always necessary to
watch out for the main point amid speculations on military
matters, theology, foreign affairs, astronomy or whatever
happened to be exercising the major's mind at the moment.

In his role as editor-in-chief the late Major Vivion de Valera liked to make unexpected swoops on the newsdesk to ensure that the NCOs and the troops remained alert. I've forgotten the topic that was being elucidated for me when this impromptu shot was taken with a telephoto lens by one of my photographer colleagues observing the scene from the end of the big room. (Picture: *Irish Press*)

Máire Comerford was one of several reporters of the early *Irish Press* who had taken part in the fight for independence and, as the house style insisted, "remained on the Republican side" in the civil war. Here, on her retirement, she receives a presentation from the then editor of the *Irish Press*, Joe Walsh. Left to right: Matt Farrell (news editor), Gerry Lawlor (reporter); Pat Murphy (reporter); WJ Redmond (managing editor); Sean Cryan (crime reporter); Máire Comerford; Kevin Collins (reporter); George Kerr (night news editor); Joe Walsh (editor); Liam Ryan (reporter); Liam Flynn (pictures editor); Brendan Ryan (reporter); and Paddy Molloy (High Court reporter). (Picture: *Irish Press*)

The late Maurice Liston ("Liston of Knockaderry," as he usually styled himself) was one of the best-loved journalists of his generation. A pioneer NUJ activist, he served as agricultural correspondent of the *Irish Press* for many years and was happiest when on the road and within easy range of country hostelries like this one.
(Picture: Douglas E Duggan)

The Joe Lynch libel action in February 1989 coincided with the Ayatollah Khomeini's death sentence on Salman Rushdie for writing *The Satanic Verses*. After the trial *Phoenix* came out with this cartoon captioned: "Look on the bright side, O'Toole, you could have libelled Mohammed."

The late Paddy Clare receiving a retirement presentation from editor Tim Pat Coogan. The legendary "night town" reporter of the *Irish Press* for over forty years, he was a veteran of the war of independence, the civil war and the Spanish civil war, where he fought with the International Brigade. He hated having to go out on stories, and on 8 December, 1954, when word came that the Tolka had burst its banks, Paddy declared: "Someone is going to have to go out on this—and my shoes are leaking."
(Picture: *Irish Press*)

With two other Irish air correspondents in Seattle, Washington, for the biggest aviation story of the decade, the roll-out of the first Boeing 747 "Jumbo" jet on 30 September, 1968. Left to right: John Healy (*Irish Independent*); Aer Lingus hostess Mary Frayne; Jack Fagan (*Irish Times*); and Michael O'Toole (*Irish Press*).
(Picture: Aer Lingus)

I took this snapshot of *Irish Press* reporters Maureen Browne and Kevin Marron in the front office in Burgh Quay in 1968 shortly after Maureen and I were married. Kevin, who went on to become editor of the *Sunday World,* was tragically killed in an air crash in Sussex sixteen years later.

Tossing pancakes on Shrove Tuesday is sometimes part of the Dubliner's Diary columnist's duties. On the right is my first friend in journalism, Frank Corr, formerly of the *Limerick Weekly Echo* and now editorial director of Jemma Publications.

At this 1966 farewell party in the Silver Swan for *Evening Press* deputy news editor Gerry Murphy were (left to right): the late Sean Lynch; Pat Chatten; the late Frank Nealis; Dermot McIntyre; Liam Flynn; Colm Brennan, now with RTE; Gerry Murphy; Michael O'Kane; Paddy Clancy; the late Conor O'Brien, editor, *Evening Press*; the late Terry Doorley; Dick Grogan, now with the *Irish Times*; Tom Fallon; the late Sean Cryan; the late WJ Redmond; (seated) Liam O'Neill, now political editor, *Cork Examiner*; the late Brendan Ryan; Micheline McCormack, now assistant editor and women's editor *Sunday World*; Aine Copeland; Peggy Larkin; and Olive Dunne.

At an *Evening Press* party in Sean Kinsella's Mirabeau restaurant to celebrate 25 years of Dubliner's Diary. Left to right: Sean Ward (editor, *Evening Press*); the late Conor O'Brien (former editor *Evening Press* and then editor, *Sunday Independent*); the late Major Vivion de Valera (editor-in-chief); the late John O'Donovan (former chief sub-editor); Sheamus Smith (film censor and a former Dubliner's Diary cameraman); the late Terry O'Sullivan; Rev Jack Brennan SJ, who served with Terry O in the army; Douglas Gageby (founding editor, *Evening Press* and then editor, *Irish Times*) and Tim Pat Coogan (editor, *Irish Press*).
(Picture: *Irish Press*)

On this occasion he delivered himself of a lengthy warning on the inherent pressures and dangers of the journalistic life. He spoke with affection of the recently deceased Terry O'Sullivan (they had been brother officers during "The Emergency") and how the strains of the journalistic life had affected him. As the major brought the interview to a close it occurred to me that there had been no main point.

I was wrong. As I was shutting the door, the major smartly called out my name. I turned to find him standing, military fashion, behind his table. "Mick," he said with some emphasis, "never forget that the kind word is the best word."

This injunction represented Major de Valera's thinking on Dubliner's Diary. At the time I thought it cockeyed and lethal—and to an extent I still do. But I'm not as sure now as I was then.

Social columns and gossip columns are rooted in man's terrible fear of missing out—the kind of fear for which, according to St Mark's gospel, Jesus gently rebuked Martha. It is given expression every night of the week at countless cocktail parties by people whose nervous eyes rake the room desperately trying to discover whether there is someone more important or more desirable to talk to than the person they happen to be talking to at the moment.

Most of those who scan the social columns and the gossip columns do so out of a misguided sense of loss. They believe there is something out there that they are missing: that there exists a vibrant and exciting sub-world peopled by those who are at once handsome, interesting and famous, and that these people are constantly partying, dining, jetting and disporting themselves seven days a week. Some readers believe that social columns are privy to these private lives and that what is published therein is an accurate—well, mainly accurate—account of them.

This, of course, is a fallacy for such a world exists only in the minds of certain columnists and their readers. It is true that in every major city there is a tiny minority who in some ways approximate to the idea of the socialites so beloved of the columnists. But these people generally go to great lengths to keep their activities private. A social columnist would not be welcome at one of their parties. The routine social events to which social columnists and gossip columnists are invited are, more often than not, commercial, repetitive and unexciting. And this leaves newspapers with a dilemma because devotees of this kind of column have a voracious appetite for fresh wonders and are fiercely intolerant of any slacking at the social mills.

The options for the hard-pressed columnist are few. He (or she) can pretend to be part of that tight and tiny magic circle. He can (as the late John Feeney of the *Evening Herald* frequently did) resort to sheer invention. He can (as nearly all of us do when pressed) put on what is known in the trade as "topspin"—the journalistic art of making silk purses out of sows' ears—hyping routine commercially oriented receptions and dubious award presentations. Or he can try to maintain a balance by attending to what he regards as the genuine social functions that come his way, avoiding the brazenly bogus and making up the slack with a ragbag of comment, humour and novelty. It was this latter option that I chose.

Without wanting to sound pious about it, I must say this was not the easiest of options. Dubliner's Diary is many things to many people: to an ad man or a PR man it represents the ideal orchard for a juicy puff; to a marketing department it appears as an especial Valhalla where readers may find relief from the unpleasantness of the news pages and indulge themselves on the succulent—if unhealthy—journalistic diet known as "a good read." (In journalistic terms, the euphemism "a good read" normally stands for material which people would like to be true even if it isn't. The first mention of that cliché should cause every real journalist to release the safety catch on his metaphorical revolver.) To the journalist who is even half serious about his craft it represents a large blank space into which on five evenings of every week must be put around 1,300 words above which his name and his photograph will appear and over which words, presumably, he feels able to stand.

The only piece of market research I ever saw concerning the column declared that it was a unique item in the paper with an overall appeal to men and women. It was, this survey insisted, "usually perceived to be concerning RDS, wine and cheeses (i.e. high society gossip column)" and this report reinforced my belief that people when confronted by market researchers tend to answer as they believe they are expected to answer. For whatever else it may have been, Dubliner's Diary never was "a high society gossip column."

But it is, I like to think, something of an Irish institution if only for the photographs of thousands of coiffured ladies and Louis Copeland-accoutred gentlemen immortalised in their moments of social triumph and for the millions of words long sunk into nothingness but once so avidly devoured and carefully weighed by those most intimately concerned with them.

Dubliner's Diary was, in the equestrian terminology of its founder, Terry O'Sullivan, "by Kilroy out of The Unknown." Kilroy was the collective pseudonym of the dozen or so reporters who contributed to the paper's first diary. Out of this ruck emerged Terry O'Sullivan, who was to carry out the experiment of going out with a photographer to conduct a nightly social round, returning during the small hours to write up the several functions covered and to develop and print the photographs.

In the Kilroy days a junior reporter named Sean Ward was sent to Dublin Airport to do a diary paragraph about a Mr Jimmy Edwards who, the Aer Lingus passenger list said, was travelling from London to Dublin on a trusty DC3. Young Ward stood by the exit but the famous moustache failed to materialise. He phoned the news editor, Jack Smith, and told the chief that he must have missed the great man. Never mind, said the kindly news editor, just write an anodyne paragraph to say he had arrived. Young Ward , chastened, duly obeyed...

The following day he found himself at the centre of a storm. The first edition of *Evening Herald* came in with a photographic reproduction of his Kilroy diary piece and the commentary that its new contemporary was quite wrong in suggesting that Mr Jimmy Edwards, comedian, flew into Dublin the previous day. Mr Edwards, the *Herald* was pleased to confirm, was playing Blackpool last evening and when telephoned by their reporter, was much amused by the story of his bilocation. Added to this was the entirely rational explanation that the Mr Edwards who landed in Dublin last evening was not Mr Edwards the comedian, but Mr Edwards an esteemed staff member of the *Evening Herald*. The *Herald*'s piece was written in such a way as to convey that the contents of its new contemporary should not always be taken at face value.

The editor, Douglas Gageby—although he has forgotten the incident—was enraged. "Fire Ward," he ordered—and fired the future editor would have been if the contrite news editor hadn't owned up and taken responsibility.

Terry O always claimed that he was not the first to try the experiment of the nightly social round, that there had been a man ahead of him who was dispatched in a taxi with a bundle of invitations and never returned to the office, phoning in several weeks later asking that his holiday money be sent on.

O'Sullivan was to become one of the most lionised journalists of his day, and was surrounded by the kind of mystique and adulation that Gay Byrne endures today. And like Gay Byrne, he erected an impenetrable shield to separate the public image from the private person.

There was much of the actor in him. He loved the limelight and adopted Oscar Wilde's dictum that a man's first duty in life is to strike a pose. In my mind's eye I see him performing his way through countless boring receptions, sniffing the air as he makes his grand entrance, hands deep in blazer pockets, sad grey eyes scanning the room, antennae finely tuned to pick up the merest hint of a slight to his majesty.

I liked him enormously and, I believe, he liked me. Terry O'Sullivan taught me the most important lesson that a journalist has to learn—that in this life there is no black and no white, only grey, and that the only thing of which one can be certain is that there is nothing of which one can be certain.

He was a mass of contradictions. An imperious sophisticate, he could—and frequently did—deliver devastating put-downs of Waugh-like savagery. Yet he was capable of extraordinary kindnesses. He was a bohemian— yet he had served as an army officer and had some of the attributes of the most snobbish of that species. Chauffeur- driven (he often claimed that he was entitled to membership of the Federation of Irish Employers) and with an entrée to the best restaurants and hotels, he sometimes didn't have enough cash in his pocket to buy the most modest of fish- and-chip suppers.

His combination of stage sense and a prose style that in the weariness of the late evening frequently tended towards the purple proved to be an irresistible mixture and his column made an incalculable contribution to the success of the *Evening Press*. In the end it added to our difficulties because his ghost haunted us. Jack Fagan of *The Irish Times* once introduced me to someone at a party saying: "This is Mick O'Toole, Terry O'Sullivan's vicar and visible head on earth."

Jack's joke, though entirely without malice, was uncomfortably near the bone. Good actor that he was, Terry O's exit was perfectly timed. I was the one left to face a changed and more demanding audience—and I had to make do with his old script and props.

Terry O paid me two fine compliments: he entrusted me with his magnificent sheepskin coat, and he asked me to write his obituary.

He dearly loved the sheepskin coat. It was at least two sizes too big for him and he sauntered about in it with all the aplomb of Anew McMaster making his first entrance as King Lear. One bitter winter evening he had this magnificent coat beside him on a stool in the Silver Swan when I came in wearing an ancient grey gaberdine which I had bought from Michael Hand for ten shillings and which, I believe, was the garment in which the future editor of the *Sunday Independent* had set out from Drogheda to make his fortune. I was very excited because on the following morning I was making my first trip to Chicago.

I listened attentively to Terry O's many recollections of the windy city.

"Do you know that there is a lake in Chicago and at this time of year it is covered with ice several feet thick?" Terry O asked rather solemnly.

I said I had read that the ice was so thick on Lake Michigan at the moment that it was possible to drive over it.

Terry O took a sip of his Powers Gold Label. "And do you know that the icy winds that sweep down from Lake Michigan are the winds that are believed to be responsible for the extinction of a species known as the brass monkey?" asked the wise one.

These winds, he went on, were capable of cutting short

the career of any young man wearing an overcoat as threadbare as mine. "Take this one," he said, proffering his prized possession.

For years Terry O shared a page with J Ashton Freeman whose Wild Wisdom column occupied one corner. On the evening of J Ashton Freeman's sudden death the editor decided that Terry O should write a tribute to him which would appear in the Wild Wisdom format in the usual place. There was, I believe, little love lost between the joint columnists but Terry O did as he was told. That evening in the Swan Terry O said to me: "I hope you'll be the one to put me down. When the time comes go to Tommy McCann in the library and you'll find that I've left the bare details for you there in my envelope. I don't much mind what you say, provided that you're not smarmy."

He then struck his number three pose which involved a gentle double rotation of the fine silver head through an arc of about 140 degrees and, having swallowed the last of his Powers Gold Label, walked out without another word.

For twenty years I resisted the temptation to open the envelope. Then, when it was clear to everyone that he was dying, I found that it contained the barest biographical details.

All obituaries are difficult but the obituaries of journalists—even the humblest of journalists—are unusually so. It seems that whenever a journalist dies his colleagues feel an overpowering urge to open the floodgates and allow the tides of hyperbole, cliché and hagiography to combine in a fulsome torrent which must appear overpowering to the laity.

Terry O deserved better of us than this and I wrote his obit as objectively and honestly as I could. I was prepared to make one exception on his behalf. I felt that having occupied the diary page almost since the foundation of the paper that his obit should appear there rather than in the news pages. I had some difficulty in persuading Sean Ward (who shares my disdain for excessive tributes to dead journalists) but ultimately he agreed and the piece appeared there with a splendid picture of Terry O receiving a Journalist-of-the-Year award.

Terry O'Sullivan came to professional journalism at the ripe old age of forty and that may explain why he never quite lost his wonder of it. His real name was Tomás Ó Faoláin. Looking round for a pseudonym when he started broadcasting in the early 1940s he asked his father-in-law if he could use his name.

He started his working life as a teacher but travel became a passion and he abandoned the classroom for a job as a courier with the Hungarian tourist board. By 1939 he was in the army as an "Emergency" man and commissioned. Then with Hitler safely seen off he drifted into the infant Irish tourist industry and started to do part-time broadcasting.

He joined the company in 1950 at the invitation of the then general manager, Sean Lemass, and thus began a love affair with the old black art that was to go on until his death. The first time I heard his name must have been soon after this. At home in Hospital I was playing with friends and coming in for high tea one summer evening their mother, a delightful woman called Nora Gaughran, commanded us all to silence pointing to the wireless saying: "Whist—here's Terry O'Sullivan from New York."

And while I remember nothing of what he said on that lovely summer evening long ago, his name would always remain in my memory. When I eventually arrived in Burgh Quay he was the most famous columnist in Ireland, cock of the walk, terror of uninitiated PR folk and confidant of editors. He and Conor O'Brien are the only people I ever heard address the Major by his first name. He, in turn, was addressed by them not as Terry but as Tom.

He was chauffeur-driven, not because of any unseemly display of appreciation or grandeur on the part of the management, but purely because of the reluctance of the insurance industry to continue covering the risk. He would take off from Burgh Quay sitting imperiously in the back seat of his car (he deplored the practice of Fianna Fáil ministers of sitting beside their drivers) and usually attending to his correspondence with the aid of a special reading light that had been installed for the purpose.

In those days he might attend up to five functions per evening. At each of these he would be plied with a glass of Powers Gold Label. No one would dare offer him a small one but he paced himself well and caused the deaths of more aspidistras than any other man in Ireland. He demanded instant recognition and instant attention. Even the slightest social solecism could attract merciless retribution. Once, after a long journey, he scandalised a hotel manager who forgot to feed him with the line: "On the way home we ate an apple." He covered birthday parties, anniversary parties, engagement parties and dress dances.

He once told me that in the dance season he sometimes stood to attention for the national anthem in Clery's, the Metropole and the Gresham all in the same evening.

At around closing-time he would return to Burgh Quay and retire to either the Silver Swan or the White Horse for what he described as "the bland cooling-off of a couple of pints of Guinness." Then with a six-pack of Guinness and a powerful short-wave radio beside him and a bottle of Powers Gold Label in his locker, he would start writing or, as he described it, making love to "Mistress Olivetti." Once started he could not be deflected. During the great feminist fervour of the late Sixties a bra-less member of staff burst into his room and, pulling up her sweater, exposed her breasts to the ageing columnist. "Absolutely splendid," said an appreciative Terry O. "Now please put them away, my dear, because there's a thousand words to go and the deadline approaches."

He was subject to and accepted lavish hospitality. His office was often littered with silver salvers and wine bottles that were regularly dispatched in the early hours from the Mirabeau in Sean Kinsella's Rolls Royce. When he travelled by train the protocol was not—with the exception of the state coach—dissimilar to that involving a journey by the President. The platform from which he boarded would have been specially cleaned that morning, the station master would be on hand to escort him to his reserved section, and a senior press officer, almost invariably Frank Finn, would travel with him. At the other end his chauffeur-driven car or a hired limousine would be awaiting him at the platform.

He was married to a brilliant woman who had a drink problem and there was a companion of long standing known as "the lady." The lady was a decent soul who didn't share Terry O's ability to hold strong drink. Sometimes there would be altercations in the back of the diary car and the lady would attack with a shoe. Terry O's response to these usually unsuccessful assaults was to whistle operatic arias and instruct the driver: "To Grangegorman... the lady is having a nervous breakdown."

Once when he was on a trip to Limerick to write about an antique fair "the lady's" aim proved more accurate than usual and Terry O alighted outside Cruise's Hotel with a bloodstained handkerchief applied to a laceration on his head. "The lady," her beehive in disarray and the mascara blotted by her tears, continued to berate him as they were received by the committee. The official greeter was so stunned by the sight that it took several moments for him to find voice. Then by way of an ice-breaker he said: "Are you interested in antiques, Mr O'Sullivan?"

"Yes, indeed," replied Terry O. "I rarely travel without one."

When Terry O died in 1980 I was assistant features editor of the *Evening Press*. I had been a regular deputy on the diary for about fifteen years and the opportunity of taking over the principal column in the paper appealed to my vanity.

There were, of course, obvious disadvantages: the tyranny of attending several social functions and producing 1,300 coherent words five evenings a week is enough to frighten off most contenders. In my case there were two other considerations: the problem of following in the footsteps of a man who was a near legend and coping with the kind of social activity that the job entails. I am essentially a shy person with a poor line in small talk. While I am gregarious and voluble in the company of friends, I have always found receptions of the kind Dubliner's Diary covers difficult and unnerving. I have never been able to master the technique of flitting from person to person at these receptions and even now I never quite know what to say to people when I meet them casually.

The workload involved was enormous. The Londoner's Diary column in the *Evening Standard* was roughly the same length as our column when I took over but it then had a permanent staff of seven journalists. Dubliner's Diary was—and remains—a one-man band.

But what really decided it for me was the fact that I seemed to be spending my entire career as somebody's deputy. For almost eight years I had been Dermot McIntyre's deputy on the newsdesk and for two years I had a similar role in the features department. I was forty-two that year and I felt like some ageing curate who desperately wants a parish.

So I wrote Terry O's obituary and took over his column. And in no time at all Terry O was writing my obituary from the grave.

As always, it is easy in retrospect to see the mistakes and how they came to be made. Sean Ward decided on a "softly, softly" transition—so soft, I felt, that the readers might be lulled into believing that Terry O was not dead but sleeping. I agreed to this. Sean also decided that no publicity or promotion should be given to the change-over. On the day I took over Dubliner's Diary two new columns—Frankie Byrne's Dear Frankie and John Boland's Earwicker—started in the paper and both were given hefty promotional publicity. Mike Murphy, then occupying the afternoon show slot on RTE Radio 1, invited me on his show to discuss the diary. Sean advised that I decline—and I did.

My view of Dubliner's Diary then—and now—is that it is a column that should report and comment on the social and cultural life of Dublin, that it should be well written, that it should not trade in gossip about people's private lives when this is likely to cause injury or distress, that it should generally (though not always) look on the bright side of things, that it should not be enslaved by commercial considerations and, most important of all, that its stories should be accurate. I also believe that it is necessary for the diarist to put his own stamp on the column and for better or worse give it, as Patrick Kavanagh said, the flavour of his personality.

I knew this would not easily be achieved. Terry O had built up a huge and loyal readership, a sizeable section of which had grown into middle age with him and with the *Evening Press*. This was an important constituency and must not be offended. More importantly, new forces—some good, some bad—had a whole decade in which to take root in Irish journalism. By 1980 the kind of column Terry O pioneered and wrote had, in the eyes of many, become *passé*.

Tony O'Reilly's regime in Middle Abbey Street was by

now well established and the *Evening Herald* was undergoing metamorphosis. The stodgy old broadsheet was being turned into a brash tabloid and a major force in this process was a likeable, exuberant and frequently irresponsible journalist with a track record as a student agitator of the Sixties. John Feeney stomped through his short life stirring pots, ruffling feathers and being generally incorrigible. The *Herald*'s social column was called Town Talk and had for years been written by Tom Hennigan, a kindly man who in the early days of what was then a ferociously nationalistic *Sunday Press* wrote a caption for a line drawing of the Manchester Martyrs in the dock which read: "The Manchester Martyrs begging for mercy after they were sentenced to death..." Tom's *Herald* column was a competent and innocuous account of the previous evening's social events. After he died it was decided to bring in John Feeney to stir the pot.

John Feeney died along with his editor, Niall Hanley, and seven others in the Beaujolais race air crash in Sussex in November 1984. He was a catalyst in Irish journalism. While feigning great rage and righteous indignation, he saw the diary page as a long giggle and churned out amazing stories about politicians, so-called socialites and captains of industry with almost total disregard for facts. Drama and intrigue were injected where neither existed.

People were reported as being at functions they had never attended. A big-name hooley in the Green Isle Hotel, Clondalkin, was described as having been "a noisy, rowdy affair" and then it transpired that he had mixed up the dates and written the piece a week before the function was due to take place.

John's report from the funeral of Princess Grace in Monaco contained an item about a row involving Frank Sinatra. "The fierce rows that have taken place in Hôtel de Paris until dawn," he wrote, "included Mr and Mrs Frank Sinatra who in my presence argued about seating arrangements with Grimaldi officials..." Other newsdesks then set to following up this juicy morsel and it transpired that Mr and Mrs Sinatra were in California and wouldn't be attending the funeral.

At one period John ran a string of stories about the Fine Gael minister Gemma Hussey, most of them casting her in a poor light. She was reported as being at parties she didn't even know were on. She was said to be holidaying in Marbella, "playground of the rich," when in fact she had never been to Marbella in her life. The stories became so persistent that Ms Hussey used to circulate a list of the inaccuracies to colleagues in Leinster House.

John's approach to diary-writing was the epitome of the "good read" philosophy and a brilliant commercial success. All attempts at criticism were laughed off. The reality, he would say, was that people read these columns only for entertainment and amusement and didn't expect what they read in them to be strictly true. That was what "a good read" meant.

The *Herald* diary soon became the most notorious column in Irish journalism and this, naturally, created pressure on me. Sean Ward wouldn't for one minute countenance the kind of reporting John was doing, yet he was naturally looking over his shoulder at what was proving to be a hot commercial property. In fairness to Sean Ward and to *Irish Press* management, I have to say that it was never even hinted to me that I should go down the same road.

But I was rapidly losing heart. I felt I wasn't putting my stamp on Dubliner's Diary to the extent that I thought I should. The fact that there was an unwillingness to promote me as the new author of the column was a blow to my confidence. (This reluctance to promote me was seized upon by the opposition, who put the story about that I was really only a stand-in.) The ghost of Terry O was unlaid.

While I felt that the diary I was producing was well written, accurate and readable I believed that something was missing. Eventually I told Sean Ward that I felt it wasn't working out and I would like out of it. Sean was sympathetic but I could see that he was relieved. I made two suggestions: I urged him to look for a bright young woman reporter and to market her and the column like baked beans.

Then as the weeks dragged on and no replacement had been found, I changed my mind. I have always hated leaving a task unfinished. Why, I asked myself, should I walk away from this one. Surely the thing to do was to rethink one's approach and go in with all guns blazing.

Sean Ward wouldn't hear of it. He was negotiating with Joe Kennedy, founding editor of the *Sunday World* and was excited at the prospect of having Joe on the team. He told me he was "relieving me of my responsibilities" in regard to the diary and that I was to return to the features department as a features writer. I was hurt but at my age and with my experience I should have known better than to resign. Later in the front hall I bumped into a colleague who was taking the new diarist to lunch and when he saw me he turned the other way. The rebuff, typical of what goes on in newspaper offices, needled me. At that moment I decided to be the General MacArthur of Dubliner's Diary. I would return.

It took four years. I started my campaign almost immediately even though it meant eating a fairly large portion of humble pie. I told the features editor that I would have no objection to deputising for the new diarist as I did for Terry O in the old days. This would allow me to write the Saturday diary each week. I was determined that it would shine.

When I returned full-time to Dubliner's Diary in August 1987 many things had altered.

Terry O's ghost had finally been laid and his chauffeur had been made redundant. Joe Kennedy, after a two-year stint, departed and rejoined his old stable, Independent House. My friend John Boland had then taken over the column. John Feeney's tragic death brought to an end the *Herald*'s excursion to the land of make believe.

The thinking behind the diary was changing to allow it to evolve both in content and appearance. Under John Boland the old social round had almost been abandoned in favour of comment pieces.

It was easier for me to make changes now. I have always believed in the dictum of Arthur Christiansen (the famous editor of the *Daily Express*) that "you can describe things with the pen of a Shakespeare himself but you cannot beat news in a newspaper." I tried to chase down valid diary-type stories and I had some successes. (The gift of a fabulous diamond necklace to Maureen Haughey, wife of the Taoiseach, by a member of the Saudi-Arabian royal family was one of these and created quite a sensation at the time.) I tried to ensure that the column was well written and that it concentrated mainly on the social and cultural life of Dublin.

And I established a little stable of hobby-horses that could be trotted out on slack evenings when there was nothing much to write about. That is how NAANA (the National Association for the Abolition of National Awards) was born. NAANA had its headquarters in Hackball's Cross. I had been elected life-president and I was supported by a council which contained some of the best-known names in the country but who couldn't, for obvious reasons, allow their names to be published.

The sheer physical workload apart, the worst part of the diary is coping with the cloying flattery of some of those who want favours. Reporters operate in both a buyer's and a seller's market and, like all buyers, are open to flattery. It is inevitable in a job like mine that there are often times when you feel like an old sow who has more piglets than she has teats for.

Sometimes when I give talks in the journalism colleges I am led to believe that I have a reputation for hating the PR industry and all it stands for. This is untrue. What I do believe is that PR should be seen as a function separate from and frequently incompatible with journalism and not as part of it.

There are other minor irritations: no one really believes that going to all those parties might possibly be construed as real work; no one takes anything you write or say seriously, and most people—colleagues and readers alike—believe themselves capable of writing a far better column than yours. For in the end we diarists are the clowns of the newspaper circus.

Did Terry O see himself as such? I don't know. He did, I believe, know a great deal about himself but for the rest of us there was always that impenetrable wall. He was the most stylish, the most enigmatic and the most acutely sardonic of all the journalists I have met. And one of the most courageous. During his last illness he kept travelling and making love to Mistress Olivetti almost until he hadn't the strength to depress the keys. Frankie Byrne visiting him in the Meath a few days before his death promised to return on Tuesday. "I'll try to be here, Frankie," he said. I had to go to New York that weekend and couldn't go to his funeral. On the Jumbo I thought of Lake Michigan and Terry O's sheepskin coat. I felt very sad. And then, 35,000 feet over the Atlantic, I could hear his voice. "Come, come, young man. We mustn't be like this. Order champagne."

8

BATTLES LOST AND WON

He's a cheery old card, grunted Harry to Jack,
As they slogged up to Arras with rifle and pack...
But he did for them both by his plan of attack.

Siegfried Sassoon, "The General"

By the start of the Seventies the fundamental flaws that within two decades would bring Irish Press Ltd. to the brink of disaster and break the absolute control of a section of the de Valera family were building up like unseen cracks in the fuselage of an aircraft.

The effective management of the three newspapers was in the hands of two men—Major Vivion de Valera, the controlling director, and the general manager, Jack Dempsey. Together they had achieved great things. The *Evening Press* was regarded as the publishing success of the decade. The *Sunday Press* was the unrivalled leader in its field.

Both men were distinguished publishing figures—there could be no dispute about that. But they were ageing. At the start of the decade Jack Dempsey was sixty-two and had been a senior executive for thirty-six years. When he finally retired due to ill-health in 1977 he had been general manager for thirty-five years. Vivion de Valera was fifty-seven in 1970 and had been controlling director and editor-in-chief since 1951.

The Major's rule was authoritarian and paternalistic. His counsels were few and his word was law. Editors and executives who had clashed with him rarely tasted victory. Although he was a just man, most of his staff found him severe and intimidating. He had the academic's bent for disputation—and an academic's keenness to come out best at it.

As far as we journalists were concerned the general manager was a far more remote figure. Although he and I spent thirteen years in the same company, we never met and I never even spoke to him on the telephone. Colm Traynor, who was for many years personnel manager and eventually succeeded Dempsey, was a modest, civilised and patient man on whom fell the onerous task of dealing with the trade unions. Ultimately, real power was in the hands of Major de Valera.

At the close of their careers both Vivion de Valera and Jack Dempsey were ill. And it was towards the close of their careers that the huge challenge created by the regeneration of Independent Newspapers by Tony O'Reilly came into its full force.

The early years of the *Irish Press* had been characterised by an odd mixture of passion, devotion, intrigue and penury. Many of the earlier figures worked with the zeal of missionaries—which is what they felt they were. This view may be all too simplistic but I have long been convinced that at least some of the reasons for the appalling tradition of industrial relations in the *Irish Press* may be traced to its first leading article and especially to the line: "We are not the organ of an individual or a group or a party." There were many whose response to that was to quote the Duke of Wellington: "If you believe that you will believe anything." It helped, I think, to create a "nudge-wink" culture in Burgh Quay.

That such a culture existed during my time there is indisputable. Aided by productivity agreements that were in many respects bogus, the flight from reality gained momentum throughout the Seventies.

The slights and the penury of the early years had a lasting effect on most of the old hands, who, in turn, passed it on to some of those who came after them. Even during the relatively affluent years of the Seventies, the *béal bocht* still haunted many quarters of Burgh Quay. Paddy Cregan, a veteran of the Thirties and for many years the group circulation manager, used to talk wistfully of "the year we were put off the train"—a reference to the successful campaign by directors of the *Irish Independent* to have the newly founded *Irish Press* excluded from the special newspaper train. Too long a sacrifice can do more than make a stone of the heart: it can erode self-confidence and self-esteem. And many of those who worked in Burgh Quay were asked to make a very long sacrifice indeed.

Getting the *Irish Press* accepted as a serious newspaper by people outside of the Fianna Fáil fold was a huge problem—and a wearying one. WJR often recalled the insults showered on those early reporters as they attempted to extract even routine information from people who regarded them as agents of the devil. This kind of prejudice lasted well into my own time. I am not likely to forget the response of the Fine Gael Minister for Finance, the late Gerard Sweetman, when I phoned him for a comment on some matter of the day. "I have certain principles in life," he said, "and one of them is never to speak to the *Irish Press*." Canon Punch, the famous parish priest of Mungret, Co Limerick, was less subtle. "I'm damned if I'll talk to any printer out of the *Irish Press*," he shouted down the phone at me and promptly hung up. The paper was frequently attacked in the Dáil. The President of the Executive Council, WT Cosgrave, asked if he intended suppressing the subversive rag, replied that there was no need to as it would soon suppress itself. Dr Noël Browne, who had a particularly active bee in his bonnet about the *Irish Press*, referred to it as *Pravda*. But the Cosgrave government did act against the paper by embarking on an astonishingly ill-advised prosecution of the editor, Frank Gallagher, before a military tribunal on a charge of seditious libel.

Gallagher was respected, even revered, by his staff and the manner of his departure after only four years caused an upheaval among the journalists which must have had long-term consequences. Most felt that he had been badly treated by the founder, and included in his personal papers is a bitter letter from Maureen Kennedy, his secretary. "I can't and won't forgive de Valera," she wrote, "he let you down badly, and as for Vivion, he is despicable—all that

underhand, furtive dealing and never to say a word." Anna
Kelly, the indomitable woman's page editor and mother
of Ruth Kelly, resigned in protest. Others, less judgemental
or more cautious, wrote to express their regret. Carl O'Daly
(better known later as Cearbhall Ó Dálaigh) was one of
these. Jack Grealish, the news editor, said in his note that
he regarded Gallagher not only as the best editor in Ireland
but in the world. The tribute was not only extravagant
but amazing—rare is the editor who is a hero to his news
editor.

The treatment of Gallagher by Harrington and
ultimately by the board helped to strengthen the inevitable
management-editorial divide which exists to some extent
in all newspapers but which has especially bedevilled the
Irish Press. To this day many editorial executives in Burgh
Quay find it difficult to identify with management
although they are as much part of management as is the
chief executive. During the 1990 crisis which almost closed
the company the NUJ chapel voted no confidence in the
management and every executive at the meeting supported
the motion.

Yet it is possible that some future historian of the *Irish
Press* may be able to demonstrate that the belligerent Mr
Harrington saved the *Irish Press* from extinction. According
to Bill Sweetman, another distinguished editor of the *Irish
Press* who also parted company with Major de Valera,
Harrington did three good things for the paper and several
bad ones.

Writing on the 50th anniversary of the foundation of
the *Irish Press*, Sweetman—a barrister and by this time a

district court judge—said: "He saved quite a sum of money by reducing the margins on each side of the pages; he reorganised the deliveries to the country so that the paper arrived almost everywhere in the mornings and he initiated an excellent series of articles exposing the scandalous conditions of life in the slums of Dublin."

Most editors—Sean Ward is an exception here—are poor administrators. And even those who are talented in that direction deeply resent every minute that they have to spend away from editing their papers. Years ago Lord Beaverbrook overcame this problem by appointing a managing editor to each of his papers who would look after the administrative side of things and allow the editor to devote himself entirely to journalism. John Gordon, the bigoted Scot who edited the *Sunday Express*, described his managing editor contemptuously as "Cudlipp, my detail man."

Were things so desperate in 1933 that the board couldn't afford £5 to send a reporter to London? Even in the Thirties it was a modest enough sum—the late Brendan Malin, who was to become one of the most respected journalists of the *Boston Globe*, joined the *Irish Press* that year at a salary of four guineas a week. Or was it, perhaps, that there were people who believed it was necessary to humble a popular and powerful editor—the only professional journalist and non-de Valera to hold the title of editor-in-chief in the history of the company—and who may have been perceived as becoming that little too powerful? It is a tantalising question—but it is unlikely that it will be resolved now.

Gallagher was a meticulous man, so meticulous that he either had an eye to posterity or felt a desperate need to cover his back. He documented everything and filed everything. When he left Burgh Quay he removed his personal files and fortunately for everyone interested in the history of Irish journalism, they found their way into the National Library as the Frank Gallagher papers. Every young journalist—and especially those who aspire to the editorial chair—should read them and be grateful to this brilliant and dedicated man for such a rich legacy.

Some of his letters to Eamon de Valera are pathetically defensive. Like many an editor before and since, he had been accused of administrative failures—of being unwilling to delegate and of being hopelessly out of touch with the commercial realities of the newspaper. It is a familiar enough refrain.

It appears that de Valera did not reply to these letters— at least not in writing. Had he done so it is unthinkable that Gallagher would have omitted them from his archive. But it is interesting that de Valera, who outlived Gallagher by thirteen years, wrote in his appreciation of him: "Frank Gallagher was by no means unpractical. The positions which he held...required executive skill and judgement of no mean order."

Frank Gallagher proved yet again that as far as newspaper managements are concerned good journalists are often difficult to handle. That lesson, seemingly, was not lost on Vivion de Valera. According to Vincent Jennings, writing after the major's death in the *Sunday Press*, the major would "counsel patience to the executive who was exasperated by the brilliant writer or photographer who had made administration a nightmare. Vivion would smile and remind us that without their flair the newspapers would indeed be dull affairs."

Had Gallagher continued to edit the *Irish Press* for six or seven years—probably the ideal span for an editor to remain in control of a newspaper—it is likely that the journalist corps at Burgh Quay would have evolved differently. As things worked out, the manner of his departure laid the foundations of what would become a seemingly impregnable wall of distrust between the management and staff.

I believe the principal reason for this was the failure several decades ago to establish a tradition of sound middle management. It seems that Major de Valera, possibly sometime in the mid-Sixties, decided against a strong middle-management structure in the company. The case was certainly put to him that editorial executives— department heads such as news editors, sports editors and chief sub-editors—should have a better deal.

He failed to respond and, I believe, lost the loyalty of several of them. Many editorial executives lacked the confidence to operate effectively. Rightly or wrongly, they believed that in a really contentious situation—particularly one involving a trade union—they might not get full backing from the senior management. Some were poorly selected and, until well into the Eighties, no editorial executive had ever received as much as an hour's training in managerial or supervisory techniques.

This is a particularly serious defect in editorial

management because it follows not at all that a brilliant reporter will make a brilliant news editor or that the most meticulous sub-editor will make an effective chief sub—frequently the opposite is the case. In Burgh Quay numerous people who, though excellent at their own trade, had no talent for dealing with people ended up in jobs requiring a high degree of supervisory skill.

One doesn't need any formal training in what is now disgustingly called "human resources" to realise that a big majority of workers need to identify with some authority figure. And when a management fails to provide effective and acceptable authority figures there are always other elements that will. There is rarely a shortage of contenders for the role of counsellor in the workplace.

At one point in the 1970s union power and intransigence reached such a peak that Burgh Quay came close to anarchy. The printers were frequently on go-slows which ensured that the *Evening Press* was constantly late in the marketplace. This kind of industrial action made proof-reading virtually impossible and the papers were filled with misprints. The motto seemed to be: "It'll do."

Stoppages of one kind or another were frequent. A supervisor who worked through that period tells me that some sections of the technical staff had a "sick" roster which ensured that a specific number of overtime shifts would be made available through bogus illnesses.

At this time I was assistant news editor of the *Evening Press* with responsibility for assigning the reporters and generally supervising their work. Once when I quite civilly asked a reporter when he might be finished the routine story he was working on he replied: "Fuck off, you bore me," and resumed reading his newspaper. When I reported this up the line I was greeted with a sympathetic shrug and the words: "What can we do?"

During this period some trade-union officers had worked themselves into positions of such power that even the most senior editorial executives feared them. This flight from industrial reality was fuelled by Larkin-like rhetoric. At chapel (house branch) meetings the management was frequently referred to as "those reptiles in O'Connell Street." Paranoia raged as rational thought and reasoning went down the Liffey. Often at these meetings I would reflect on what might happen if our deliberations were going out live on RTE television. I usually came to the conclusion that the sales of all our papers would drop by at least 50 per cent on the morrow.

It would be quite wrong to give the impression that this behaviour applied across the board. It didn't—and the majority of *Irish Press* workers, then as now, were decent and rational people who wanted to do an honest and professional job. The tragedy was that a set of circumstances had combined to ensure that these reasonable, intelligent people would collectively condone behaviour and standards which as individuals they found repugnant.

Journalists and newspaper proprietors are supposed to be professional communicators, yet when it comes to their own industry they often perform as crass amateurs. For most of my time in Burgh Quay internal communications were absymal. It is only in very recent times that management has embarked on any systematic communications programme—a move much resented by many trade-union officials who hold that they should have the monopoly rights of communicating matters to the workers.

Vivion de Valera died in February 1982, his final years clouded by ill-health and the worry of the declining fortunes of the newspaper industry. Despite its early commercial promise, the previous decade had been commercially disastrous. The weariness, the fever and the fret was everywhere.

The cost of wages and newsprint had spiralled and in the first five months of 1975 the volume of advertising in the Dublin dailies dropped by an average of 26 per cent. With advertising revenue plummeting there was no way out but to continue the spiral of cover price increases which, combined with a couple of other factors, would in time have a devastating effect on the whole industry.

Crisis followed crisis as circulation figures plummeted and revenues declined. Irish Press Newspapers weren't the only sufferers. With only rare exceptions, the decline was general throughout the industry and it was persistent. In the four years 1986-1990 the sales of Irish morning papers (with the exception of *The Irish Times*) declined by 8 per cent; Irish Sundays declined by 5 per cent and Irish evenings declined by 15 per cent. By this time it was now obvious to all but the simple-minded that the newspaper industry was undergoing profound change.

On 7 July, 1989, after months of speculation, Dr Eamon de Valera, the then chairman and chief executive of *Irish Press* plc, formally announced that agreement in principle had been reached with Ingersoll Publications of New Jersey for a partnership in which Ingersoll would acquire a 50 per cent equity shareholding in *Irish Press* Newspapers, publishers of the three titles. Ingersoll was initially putting up £5m in equity and £1m by way of loan.

I was in Singapore researching a magazine article when Ralph Ingersoll II burst upon the Dublin newspaper scene but Maureen phoned me to tell me of the jubilation and she read over some of the headlines.

I knew nothing of Ralph Ingersoll II at that time. But I had read a volume of the autobiography by his famous father, another Ralph Ingersoll, a liberal New York editor and publisher of the Thirties and Forties who had an affair with the playwright Lillian Hellman and became easy prey to the McCarthyites.

When I got home and read the cuttings I could see that Mr Ingersoll had made a great impression everywhere except (surprise! surprise!) in the *Irish Independent*. Naturally enough, the *Irish Press* papers were euphoric. "The Perfect Partner" screamed the *Irish Press* headline. Under the headlines: "Ingersoll to Change Rules of Game" and (a quotation from Ingersoll) "We're committed to the papers and the nation," the then financial editor, Damien Kiberd, quoted the new joint proprietor as saying he would give Tony O'Reilly's *Independent* Newspapers "a contest they did not expect."

"We come with optimism, with capital, with know-how and with an emotional commitment both to the papers and to the nation," Mr Ingersoll was quoted as saying. Under the headline "Complete Newsman with Style of a Winner," another *Irish Press* reporter wrote: "What we have here is a newspaperman—in the fullest sense of the word." The story then quoted Ingersoll saying that "as fast as manufacturers can deliver, within six to nine months," the company would be installing state-of-the-art presses and new photographic technology—the most advanced production technology on the planet.

There were to be obstacles along the way. A new cost-cutting corporate plan drawn up under the new regime included voluntary redundancies and a five-day working week instead of the four-day week enjoyed by journalists and printers since the heady days of the Seventies. The unions offered fierce resistance to changing the four-day week. Both sides dug in. Then to the dismay and astonishment of the unions, the Labour Court backed the management's plans.

The NUJ held out. I was among the tiny minority who favoured making the concession until the company's fortunes had been turned round. I believed at that time that the company was on the brink of closure and I reckoned there was little public sympathy to be gained through insistence on a four-day week as the company was disintegrating. This was regarded as heresy by most of my colleagues. A young reporter who had recently joined the company said on RTE's *Morning Ireland* that he had forty or so working years ahead of him and he wasn't going to spend them in a sweatshop.

The board made it clear that they would close down rather than depart from this basic principle. Throughout that hot July of 1990 the pressure became almost unbearable. A compromise deal which included a four-and-a-half-day week (but with five attendances) was rejected by the unions on the grounds that it was a return to the five-day week through the back door. Finally on Friday, 20 July, Vincent Jennings, the chief executive, wrote to each staff member saying that it would not be possible to continue publication after the following Monday. That evening I saw him walking through the building, tears streaming down his face.

The first leader in the *Sunday Press* of 22 July was headed "We Hope to See You Next Sunday." It said that as the editorial was being written "the life of the *Irish Press* Group of newspapers hangs on a thread..." A few hours previously, the *Evening Press* was displaying no such optimism. Across six columns on its front page, under the headline "The Evening Darkens—A Goodbye Is Hard to Say," editor Sean Ward said definitively: "This is the last issue of the *Evening Press*. That was easier to write than it is to believe. Unfortunately, it is true." He ended by saying: "This is a sad day for all of us here. But times change. The world goes on. Goodbye and thank you." Many people said to me afterwards that it wasn't until they read Sean Ward's piece that they really realised the game was up. It certainly concentrated a large number of minds.

Fortunately for all of us, the editor was wrong. Within the next twenty-four hours a formula of words was found which allowed some people the luxury of believing that their faces had been saved. At that dramatic chapel meeting of Sunday afternoon it was actually presented to us as a victory. We had achieved nothing. All the tension, all the delirium had achieved nothing. The management's plan was implemented.

Next morning I suggested to Sean Ward that he write a follow-up article to "The Evening Darkens..." and that it should be headlined "The Evening Brightens—as the Staff Frightens." He was only slightly amused.

9

THAT OCCUPATIONAL HAZARD

No one comes out of a libel court smelling of roses.

Adam Raphael, *My Learned Friends*

"Gossip. That's what you write, Mr O'Toole, isn't it?"

Mr Colm Condon SC, icily polite, great arched eyebrows stark as bushes after a gorse fire, spat out the word "gossip" as if it were some poisonous substance he had accidentally ingested.

"Gossip," he repeated, turning towards the jury box and stressing the digraph so that the vowel sounded like the crack of a ringmaster's whip.

I was at that moment occupying what my colleague Paul Muldowney warned me was the loneliest spot in Ireland—the witness box of the number three court of the High Court of Ireland. "The middle of a Leitrim bog on All Souls' Night has nothing on this," Paul had said, patting the mahogany railing of the witness box in the empty courtroom that morning. And Paul should know. The doyen of the High Court reporting staff, he has sat through hundreds of trials and observed the majesty and the savagery of the law in all its guises. Paul is the most considerate and congenial of colleagues. Although I had spent a considerable portion of my working life in the courts, I had never attended a libel trial. Now as the defendant in what was shaping up as a major one I sought Paul out in that empty courtroom essentially to seek his advice but also to look on a friendly face.

"You know as well as I do that anything can happen in a court," Paul said. "You can only give it your best shot. Tell the truth. Keep your hands on your lap and look in the direction of the jury. Don't appear to be shifting in the box. Above all, don't let Colm Condon lure you into trying to score points off him." It was excellent advice. And having given it Paul assumed the role of impartial reporter, according me during those three traumatic days the same civil nod as he gave the opposing side. I especially admired him for that. Barristers see these things in different terms. RN Cooke SC, who led for the defence, simply said: "I'll be putting you in the witness box after lunch and Colm Condon will come at you with all guns blazing." Journalists dread libel in the way that pilots dread metal fatigue. To most of us it is the occupational hazard *par excellence*. True, there may be the odd egomaniac who relishes the notoriety of his day in the libel court. But such is very exceptional. They know the particular hazards of libel trials—that some juries may believe newspapers have unlimited resources and that in any event they are insured against libel—which they are not.

To the lawyers, libel is very often a game—and a lucrative one at that. I'm not suggesting that lawyers are totally insensitive to the human issues involved, but their approach is—and has to be—a businesslike one.

To every serious journalist, a libel action is a malpractice suit. Libel has been defined as "any defamatory matter which brings a person into hatred, ridicule and contempt." The "hatred, ridicule and contempt" bit has now been modified to lowering a person's reputation in the minds of reasonable, right-thinking people. The defamation need not be in writing, for the spoken word, or even a gesture, may come within the realm of slander. A defendant who hung a burning lamp outside a house during the day time was successfully sued because the court found that he had "marked out the dwelling house of the plaintiff as a bawdy house." Another man got damages for a claim that "while the plaintiff was seated on a bench in a public place, the defendant in the presence of three other persons lifted up his right leg in the direction of and in the immediate vicinity of the plaintiff, as if he were a dog..." It is possible, as Jonathan Swift said, to:

> Convey a libel in a frown
> And wink a reputation down.

Even at the worst of times one couldn't be hanged for a libel, although one could—and still, technically, can be— jailed for criminal libel. The old charges of criminal and seditious libel were for decades the mainstay of repressive governments. In the early nineteenth century the young Robert Peel, then the Chief Secretary for Ireland, wrote of the *Dublin Evening Post* that "most of the dissatisfaction in this country arises from the immense circulation of that nefarious paper. The editor, a Mr McGee, was duly charged with perpetrating a criminal libel on the Lord Lieutenant, fined £200 and sentenced to two years in prison."

My own case was not, I knew, going to send me to Mountjoy. But because of who was involved I suspected—and I was right—that it would become the most highly publicised Irish libel action of modern times. And it all started because Joe Lynch—Dinny of *Glenroe*—didn't go to a party. The offending article consisted of six short paragraphs totalling 273 words in the bottom of the Dubliner's Diary page in a section which every evening bore the standard headline "And While I'm At It." The story told how a group of six agricultural journalists and their guests had planned a social evening at which the organisers promised Mr Lynch would sing. Alas, Mr Lynch failed to turn up and the article quoted one of the organisers as saying that his failure to do so seemed to him to be "slightly less than professional."

Those six paragraphs were to cost the *Evening Press* £25,000 in damages and roughly the same in legal fees—in all, about £183 a word, after the jury found that they were defamatory of Mr Lynch. There was only one reason why the story had appeared in Dubliner's Diary—the old media theory that the doings of soap opera stars are of major interest to the public. Mr Condon, in the fulfilment of his professional duty, strove hard to convince the jury that there was another and a sinister reason, that the *Evening Press* had set out to "get" Mr Lynch and that we were activated by malice towards him.

Fortunately, the jury didn't buy that one. Had they done so the damages would have been many times the fairly modest £25,000 they awarded.

In 1989, when the action was heard, libel damages were going through the roof. In Britain new records were being established almost by the week. There had been a £1m out of court settlement to Elton John by *The Sun* which Mr Condon cleverly and subtly linked with our case without even naming the participants. Miss Koo Stark had been awarded £500,000; Mrs Sonia Sutcliffe, wife of the Yorkshire ripper, had been awarded £600,000 against the satirical magazine *Private Eye*, a sum later substantially reduced. Many lawyers and journalists felt that the time was right for Irish libel damages to escalate to a new record. A barrister friend told me that after the first day of the trial the figure being spoken of in the law library was £75,000. Being a natural pessimist, I threw in an extra £25,000 and convinced myself that Mr Lynch was going to get a round £100,000.

The fateful story had, as often happens, come to me through a colleague. My desk was next to that of the then agricultural correspondent, Daragh McDonnell. Daragh casually mentioned that he had been to a social organised by the Guild of Agricultural Journalists a couple of nights before where there had been great disappointment because the star turn, Joe Lynch, failed to turn up. So great was the chagrin, Daragh said, that some of the guests tore down the posters of Mr Lynch that had been placed around the room. After quizzing Daragh I made three independent checks. I first phoned Gerry O'Grady, the guild secretary. Gerry wasn't at all keen on publicity and went over the details with some reluctance. Gerry's lack of enthusiasm edged me along the road to disaster. Had he or any committee member given even the merest hint of enthusiasm for publication, I would have automatically interpreted this as axe-grinding and the fear of any possible embellishment would have caused the stall warning to sound. The substance of what Gerry told me was that Joe Lynch has agreed to perform at their function for a fee of £100; that he failed to show up on the night, and when they finally reached him by phone he told them he was tired and wet after a heavy day's filming and had to go out again the following morning. In the circumstances, he couldn't make it. This checked out with my original information. I now phoned the treasurer of the guild, David Markey, at the *Irish Farmer's Monthly*. His version of events dovetailed with the two earlier informants. It remained for me to check the story with the man himself. On the evening before publication, a Friday, I phoned his home. His wife told me he was working in the North and she had no contact number for him. In normal circumstances I would have no hesitation in killing the piece. But the circumstances were not normal because three professional journalists, each of whom had been present, had authenticated the story. I wrote the piece, ending with the line: "Mr Lynch was in the North last night and unavailable for comment." There couldn't, I reasoned, be any loophole.

There was.

The story appeared on Saturday. The following morning

a furious Mr Lynch was on the phone to the duty news editor, Jimmy Walsh, pointing out that he was not under contract to turn up at the function, that the suggestion that he would work for a fee of £100 was ludicrous and insulting, and that our allegation that he had failed to honour a commitment was damaging to him personally. He was, he told Jimmy, a reasonable man and he would consider an apology. Jimmy wrote the customary memo, thereby setting in motion the cumbersome and antiquated machinery which at that time was used to deal with potential libels. The possibility of nipping potential libels in the bud is naturally a desirable proposition as far as newspapers are concerned. Most libels are due to accident or carelessness, not malice. If only some system could be devised whereby newspapers could apologise there and then, making reasonable amends, much money and much anxiety would be spared. Unfortunately, as far as the newspapers are concerned there are hazards. For as the law stands, an apology may be construed as an admission of guilt.

When he was cross-examining me, Mr Condon made much of the fact that in all the time that had intervened I never once made an attempt to apologise to Mr Lynch. Any civilised lay person, not knowing the realities involved, might ask the same question. The reality is that any journalist who gets involved in a libel action is no longer a free agent in regard to the potential action. He becomes a prisoner of the lawyers who must sanction his every move. Proprietors vary in their attitudes to journalists who succumb to the great occupational hazard. They are not, as many people believe, insured against libel damages and almost invariably stand to lose a great deal of money. Some proprietors panic and expect the entire staff to don sackcloth and ashes. Most concentrate on minimising the potential damages and settle out of court, often with grovelling apologies and cash settlements.

Others adopt a philosophical approach. In his book *Pressures on the Press*, Charles Wintour, the distinguished former editor of the London *Evening Standard*, recalls how he wrote to his proprietor, Lord Beaverbrook, after a particularly difficult skirmish in the libel courts. Beaverbrook, who frequently submitted his editors to tongue-lashings for trivialities, replied:

> You must not make apologies for involving the *Evening Standard* or any other newspaper in a libel action. That is the risk of the profession. It is what might be called an occupational risk. There is no possibility of my complaining or making any row about these misfortunes that descend upon us if there is no negligence... Please be advised now that there is no need ever to make apologies or to be in the least upset by libel actions or similar attacks on us even though we go down for large sums.

The management of the *Irish Press* have always behaved decently towards journalists who found themselves in this kind of trouble. No more than any other businessman, Dr Eamon de Valera certainly doesn't like going down for large or even small sums. But in my case—and in every other case that I know of—no pressure was applied, no word of criticism or rebuke was spoken.

On the morning of Mr Lynch's initial complaint the duty news editor wrote the usual memo to the editor, Sean Ward. After I was told of the situation on Monday I went back to my contacts individually. As they reiterated the story a new dimension emerged. The "deal" between Mr Lynch and the Guild of Agricultural Journalists whereby he would appear for a fraction of his normal fee was negotiated not by his agent or manager, as I thought and wrote, but by a third party, a member of the staff of an advertising agency which used Mr Lynch for work on farming commercials. Even though the introduction of the Old Pals Act worried me, all my informants were adamant that there had been a definite commitment by Mr Lynch to turn up. This, as I have said, was entirely rejected by the jury.

This was to prove crucial. Mr Condon's case to the jury—which, with the exception of the charge that we had acted maliciously, was fully accepted by them—was that no contract existed; that he gave only a qualified commitment, emphasising that he would attend as a favour but only if he were free to do so and if filming commitments allowed.

In due course Mr Lynch's solicitor wrote to the editor and to me stating that he regarded the article as "a grave and malicious attack on my client's character, professional ability and integrity." The tone of the article, he claimed, implies that his client "breaks engagements with impunity and implies that my client has a complete disregard for the feelings of members of the public whether they be agricultural journalists or otherwise, when in fact my client has served members of the public in his professional capacity for many years with a zeal for correctness in every degree whether in acting or singing on Radio, State [sic] or Television." There followed the standard invitation to submit a suitable apology and the offer of a suitable sum in damages.

Mr Lynch's statement of claim was filed in the High Court four months after the article appeared. It alleged that the article was false and malicious, that it had damaged Mr Lynch in his professional reputation and brought him into ridicule and contempt. The defendants, it went on, "were activated by spite towards the plaintiff." The mills of the Four Courts, like those of the deity, grind slowly. For almost three years, I heard no more. Towards the end of this period I was told that efforts to settle had failed and we would be defending the action. A consultation with counsel was set up in the office of Elio Malocco, then a director of Irish Press PLC, and the company solicitor.

Leading for us was RN Cooke SC, veteran of many libel actions, former soldier and like his friend and brother officer, Major Vivion de Valera, a man with an academic interest in munitions. It was felt among those of my colleagues who had been afflicted by the occupational hazard that Mr Cooke had little sympathy for their plight and that he frequently regarded them as the authors of their own misfortunes. As I had never seen him, I went down to the picture library and asked for his photograph. Strangely, for a man who had served the paper as its leading counsel for thirty years or more, there was no stock photograph.

The clippings library had nothing either. I looked him up in the Law Directory and found his listing under that of his son, also a senior counsel. It said tersely that RN Cooke BComm, SC had been called to the bar in 1938, took silk in the Michaelmas term of 1959 and was made a bencher of the King's Inns in 1980. Well, I mused, we at least had 1938 in common. I was born in the year that RN Cooke was called to the bar. When he eventually came face to face in Elio Malocco's office, I found an elderly man, bald, of military bearing and with bright, quizzical eyes. He was dressed—surprisingly, I thought—in a flashy sports jacket and trousers rather than the traditional sombre suit of the profession. Whenever I looked across the room he seemed to be scrutinising me like a gourmet examining a newly opened bottle of wine which he strongly suspects to be corked. When he eventually spoke he was formal and incisive. "Tell me, Mr O'Toole," he asked, "how well do you know Mr Lynch?" With this casual question, Mr Cooke was testing for malice—which, if proven, would result in punitive damages. He appeared relieved when I replied that I knew Mr Lynch not at all and had met him only once and that for all of about twenty seconds.

The trial opened on Tuesday, 7 February, 1989. RN Cooke, wigged, gowned and bristling for the off, met me outside the law library with his junior, Elizabeth Dunne. There was a last-minute consultation with Elio Malocco and others involved in a ghastly subterranean room of the Four Courts. I got the impression that RN Cooke—like myself—wanted to settle. Colm Condon, he said, had remarked to him that this one was going to cost the *Irish*

Press a great deal of money because of the losses incurred by Mr Lynch following the publication. Elio Malocco was not in the mood for peacemaking. So RN Cooke would not be going into court asking for a strikeout and assuring the judge that "this matter need no longer trouble your lordship." As the fatal minutes ticked away it was becoming clear that one of their lordships was indeed going to be troubled.

But which one? There is a belief among simple folk that when someone puts on a judge's wig or a bishop's mitre or dons some other trappings of high office, a divinely inspired metamorphosis takes place causing prejudice and many of the other frailties of humanity to flee the mind and soul. Alas, this does not happen in the real world. Judges, as anyone who has closely followed the career of Lord Denning will know, may harbour certain prejudices. Some indeed are thought to harbour prejudices against the media.

It is one of the great ironies of a libel trial that participants are at liberty to make allegations against the defendants which, were they to be spoken outside a courtroom or other privileged location, would automatically lead to a fresh action for defamation. And it is little consolation to a litigant bearing the full brunt of such an onslaught that without such privilege there would be no justice for anyone and that the lawyer is performing an impersonal, professional duty.

Although I was aware of all these things, I was still taken aback by what I regarded as the ferocity of Mr Condon's opening speech to the jury. For it seemed to me that he set out to link me, the *Evening Press* and Dubliner's Diary in the minds of the jury with the worst muck-raking activities of the Fleet Street gutter press. Seizing on the recent libel developments in Britain, he suggested by innuendo that the *Evening Press* might have engineered the whole Lynch business so as to gain publicity for themselves! (Considering that the company was at that moment on the brink of financial ruin, this was quite an astonishing suggestion.) The story, he insisted, was a smear—the *Evening Press* had set out to "get" Mr Lynch and smear him. During cross-examination I pointed out that smearing was entirely contrary to the traditions of the company. Gossip, he insisted, was my trade. Gossip was what columns like mine were all about. Gossip and smear. Smear and gossip. I pointed out that Dubliner's Diary was not strictly a gossip column: that I had never written stories about marital breakdowns, families ravaged by alcoholism or any of the other misfortunes that may beset the well-known.

Mr Condon seemed to be attaching particular significance to the fact that the Lynch item had appeared under the headline "And While I'm At It"—a standard headline at the end of each evening's column under which odds and ends including numerous "puffs" for charities were printed. While this onslaught was going on Sean Ward had an idea. The jury had seen only photocopies of the offending piece in isolation. Why not show them copies of the entire column so that they could judge the Joe Lynch piece against the rest. Copies were made and the jury saw that the Joe Lynch item, tucked away at the bottom of the page, was preceded by stories about a new theatre for Trinity College, the painter Sir Sidney Nolan coming home to paint and a piece about a fund-raising effort by some Irish language body. It was a dull diary that evening but it certainly wasn't a malicious one.

As everyone expected, Joe Lynch was a superb witness. He told the jury of the numbness he felt when he read the article, how his initial reaction had been to say to himself "What have I done to anybody to deserve this? I am too old to get angry at things like that," he added, "but I suppose I was seething inside." As Mr Lynch was claiming a big reduction of income since the appearance of the article, RN Cooke now had to cross-examine him and his accountant on his financial affairs. Mr Cooke handled him very gently in cross-examination, teasing out the various payments for appearances and explaining to the jury the actor's contract with an Isle of Man financial institution which, as his accountant pointed out, was an arrangement whereby many entertainers and sportsmen were enabled to postpone the payment of income tax.

The trial dragged on for four days. David Markey and Gerry O'Grady, who had spoken to me about the story, gave evidence on our behalf, stating that they believed they had a definite commitment from Mr Lynch. Mr Justice O'Hanlon's summing-up was like a rose-lover's dissertation on his garden—courteous, good-humoured, patient and serious. The summing-up is a crucial aspect of every trial. Listening to one articulated by a dispassionate and careful judge can be an exhilarating experience. Gone are the rhetoric, the innuendo, the subtle intimidation that surfaces during the hurly-burly of the trial. Instead comes logic, fairmindedness and courtesy. It is as if someone had opened a window in a stifling room.

Not all litigants are lucky. Shortly before my case there had been the astonishingly partisan summing-up of Mr Justice Caulfield in the Jeffrey Archer libel case in the High Court in London. Not only did counsel for the defendants have to ask the judge to correct nine misstatements of fact in his charge to the jury but the latter further distinguished himself by paying a bizarre tribute to the wife of the plaintiff. "Remember Mrs Archer in the witness box," enthused his lordship. "Your vision of her will probably never disappear. Has she elegance? Has she fragrance?"

Grave as an eagle, Mr Justice O'Hanlon patiently reviewed the evidence. He suggested to the jury that the whole trouble might have arisen because of the rather unbusinesslike manner in which both sides approached the engagement. Even if there were an old pal's act or an obligement without fee one would have expected that Mr Lynch would have put something in his diary to remind himself. Conversely, wouldn't it have been very wise of Mr Markey and another man involved in the booking to write and thank Mr Lynch for agreeing to come? Mr Justice O'Hanlon then suggested to the jury that if they came to the conclusion that the publication was made in the justifiable belief that it was correct, then they would be entitled to take that fact into account when assessing damages.

After the last juror had filed out of the courtroom Mr Condon was on his feet claiming that there was no basis in law for such a direction. The judge agreed to recall the jury and he amended his charge on this point. It took two hours for the jury to find that the words complained of were false and defamatory. To the question: were the defendants activated by malice, the jury answered "no." They awarded Mr Lynch £25,000 damages and Mr Justice O'Hanlon entered judgement with costs.

The Joe Lynch case taught me two important lessons. I learned how painful it is to be at the receiving end of massive unwanted publicity. RTE played the story very big—it was the number two item on the main national news bulletin two evenings in a row. The morning after the case ended Gay Byrne congratulated Joe Lynch on his victory. Each evening as I left the court I was pursued by cameramen and sound men. It is a scenario I had watched countless times from the sidelines. Now I was at the centre of it and it was immensely distasteful. The second lesson is that no matter how good, how airtight or how reliable the source, I would never again take responsibility for publishing a contentious story without making contact with the subject and inviting comment.

As in all vicissitudes one is overwhelmed by the kindness of one's friends and colleagues. The case brought a large crop of letters from friends, colleagues and readers. I was particularly chuffed that Maeve Binchy noticed that I had kept the column running through the trial. This had been difficult but it was a point of principle with me.

Douglas Gageby wrote: "You must not be too downcast, it happens to all of us...it's a hazard of the game." Dean Victor Griffin of St Patrick's Cathedral wrote consolingly and counselled: "*Nil desperandum.*" Dr Anthony Clare wrote from the other St Patrick's and ended by asking if there was anything he could do. (At one point I felt so bad that there nearly was.) Tim Pat Coogan wrote: "One good thing about the attrition of newspaper work is that its ephemeral nature works in one's favour as well as against. This time next year you'll be saying, 'Case—what case?'"

Tim was right. Two years after the case I was giving a talk to a group of sixty-five people on the subject of the media and crime. There had been a discussion about the effects of publicity on crime victims. I decided to conduct an experiment. I told the group that I had been involved as a defendant in the most publicised libel case in the history of modern Irish journalism and invited those who could name the man who sued me to raise their right hands.

Out of the group of sixty-five, only one man raised his hand. He raised it hesitatingly, lowered it for a couple of seconds and raised it again. I invited him to name the plaintiff.

"I could be wrong," he said, "but was it Joe Lynch?"

10

BUSINESS IS BUSINESS

O Ireland my first and only love
Where Christ and Caesar are hand in glove!
James Joyce, "Gas from a Burner"

Most newspapers like to give the impression that they are
social institutions rather than mere businesses operating in
what has become a merciless commercial environment.
The dichotomy between social responsibility and
commercial advantage is nearly always an interesting one.
In the case of newspapers it is particularly engrossing. For
example, on 20 September, 1991 every director of *Irish
Press* plc—including the editor-in-chief and a former editor
of the *Sunday Press*—who attended that day's annual
meeting of shareholders voted to prevent RTE cameramen
from filming during the meeting. The directors were under
some pressure as they believed there was a plan by worker
shareholders to make trenchant criticisms of sensitive topics
and that the presence of TV cameras would escalate matters.

That situation and the problems it creates is as old as
television and it has had to be faced by police officers,

politicians, trade unionists, dictators, generals and businessmen alike. I imagine that most journalists would be in favour of full exposure. I certainly am, and while I was not part of any plot to attack the directors that afternoon, I voted for the cameramen to stay. I find it hard to understand how any journalist could vote differently. Eamon de Valera and Vincent Jennings had no such qualms. They are honourable and decent men. They obviously reasoned that saving an embattled company that had endured much dishonest media coverage from a potentially serious fresh attack more than justified their action.

The view of newspapers that the press likes to foster is centred on the ideals of nineteenth-century liberalism when it was shaking off the shackles of two centuries of censorship and control. That was the glorious period during which Louis Napoleon's ambassador had to report to his master after an attack in *The Times*:

Someone has told you, prince, that the hostility of *The Times* and the *Morning Chronicle* was provoked by pecuniary subsidies. Nothing could be more false than such an assertion and, believe me, on such an important subject I would not make a statement without being absolutely certain. It is possible that third-class papers like the *Sun*, *Standard*, etc. might be purchased. But the enterprise of *The Times* and *Morning Chronicle* are backed by too big capital, their political management is in too many hands for it to be possible to buy them for any price whatsoever...

And almost a century later the splendid ring of outrage

in the voice of Adolph Ochs, publisher of *The New York Times*, as he sends an insolent advertiser packing to his greasy till:

> You must excuse me from discussing the policy of *The New York Times*. It is a subject we do not care to discuss with an advertiser...You seem to wish that *The New York Times* should go about as a mendicant begging for advertising patronage. We will never do anything of the kind...

Here in Ireland there is a long and painful history of "bought" newspapers. Prof Kevin B Nowlan estimates that in the second decade of the nineteenth century, when Robert Peel dominated the Irish administration, as much as £20,000 a year was being spent by Dublin Castle to bring Irish newspapers to heel. The notion of the "kept" newspaper is still very strong in the Irish psyche. The *Irish Press* has had great difficulty in shaking off the image of being the kept newspaper of Fianna Fáil.

Years ago I knew of a newspaper in which the head of a big department store, a major advertiser, had a veto in the matter of the reporting of court cases. Indeed the history of modern journalism doesn't give the public many reasons for great trust.

In Burgh Quay Christ and Caesar were never really hand in glove. (Caesar, in fact, wasn't in Burgh Quay at all but in O'Connell Street with the rest of the big bad bunch of accountants, cashiers and administrators.) The commercial pressures of Burgh Quay were absorbed by Major Vivion de

Valera and his general manager, Jack Dempsey. Journalists rarely got involved in them, although WJ Redmond, the managing editor, frequently had to deal with an incensed shareholder who consistently complained that the Bradmola stockings advertisement was indecent. (It consisted of a five-inch line drawing of the leg—from toe to mid-thigh—of a comely maiden and with a black line down the middle to signify the seam) WJR spent hours trying to convince this shareholder that this harmless piece of commercial art wouldn't drive the youth of Éireann to irrevocable spiritual ruin nor would it have Patrick Pearse revolving in his grave.

Advertising pressures which *can* be very great in the newspaper world were never a big problem for us in Burgh Quay. Most advertisers expect and believe they are entitled to special consideration in editorial matters. And most—though by no means all newspapers—show such consideration in varying degrees.

When Harold Evans, then editor of *The Sunday Times*, started that paper's magnificent campaign for justice for thalidomide victims he phoned the general manager and asked how much Distillers, the manufacturers of the drug, spent with *Times* Newspapers. The sum, he was told, ran to many millions a year because Distillers were the company's biggest advertising client. "You won't, I know, be influenced by that—nor should you," said the general manager. Evans was lucky—his proprietors were Thomson Newspapers and Lord Thomson of Fleet supported his editors to an extraordinary degree. The Thomson family was eventually driven out of Fleet Street by intransigent and greedy trade unions. Their place was taken by Mr Rupert Murdoch.

There are some newspapers that use a subtle blackmail to attract advertising. They refuse all mention (except in the most exceptional circumstances) to companies which refuse to advertise with them. The pressures appear to have always been there. In *Ulysses* we find Mr Bloom, advertising canvasser, approaching Mr Crawford, editor, on behalf of a client who sells tea. Poor Bloom is full of enthusiasm. "He'll give us a renewal for two months...but he wants just a little puff. What will I tell him, Mr Crawford?" Mr Crawford, like many a journalist before and since, has the answer pat. "Will you tell him that he can kiss my arse. Tell him that right from the stable...he can kiss my right royal Irish arse."

Things have become far more sophisticated since Mr Bloom's day. A huge PR industry has grown up in Ireland, its major concern similar to that of Mr Bloom although, one suspects, for more rewarding fees. They would see it differently of course but puffery is what PR is chiefly about. The rise of the PR industry presents an enormous challenge—and threat—to journalism. More and more—you can detect it in the pronouncements of some members of the judiciary—certain people are coming round to the belief that newspapers should be allowed print only that which is given to them to print. That is known as "journalism by handout" and it is the negation of everything that good journalism is all about. Unchecked, it is capable of destroying our democratic processes. Good journalism is about casting a cold eye on what is going on in the world, the country, the parish. Unfortunately the PR people are making most of the running. As many newspapers weaken in the harsh economic climates in which they have to operate, the supplied story is all too welcome.

The growth of PR has hit the newspapers in another way by deflecting advertising revenue from them. The professional advice offered to many potential advertisers is to run a clever PR campaign—where the newspapers will give the publicity for free—and put the bulk of the advertising spend into TV. I have never understood how the newspapers were prepared to stand by and allow this situation to develop to the extent that it did without even having as much as a study undertaken.

Dubliner's Diary is by its very nature open to puffery; there are those who believe I would best serve the paper by turning it into a collection of puffs. My attitude from the start was to be supportive of advertisers provided the material offered was usable and accurate and that I would have final control of the material that appeared under my name. Irish Press Newspapers have as it happens a cleaner record than most in massaging the interests of advertisers. For example, the *Irish Press* was never involved in the blatant puffery of the auctioneering and property businesses.

I had extremely good relations with any of the firm's customers with whom I came in contact. I believe that the diary also has a public-relations function and I was always careful to attend customers' functions and meet them personally. Had anyone suggested to me that as a journalist I was anti-business, that I was determined to write only "knocking copy" about Dublin business interests, I would have been very, very surprised. Business communities everywhere can be notoriously sensitive—let alone demanding—on these issues and those who are in the position of calling the tune frequently have bizarre musical tastes.

Thus in the spring of 1989 I found myself the subject of the joint charges that my column was showing "persistent hostility to the business community in Dublin" and that over a period of three years I had managed to write only knocking copy about the Dublin City Centre Business Association and its prominent members. The letter, signed by the association's secretary, Tom Coffey, was marked Private and Confidential and addressed to Dr Éamon de Valera as managing director. The company was at that time going through the worst financial traumas in its history. The last line of Mr Coffey's letter said: "I hope you will do something about it." Dr de Valera sent the letter down to Sean Ward. Sean said he had no worries about the first part of the letter—a complaint about a specific piece I had written about the association—as this was comment and I was entitled to my opinion. "What do you have to say about these other charges? They certainly need answering."

The Dublin City Centre Business Association is one of Ireland's leading pressure groups. Founded in 1970 as the Dublin Night Traders' Association, it soon began to concern itself with law-and-order matters and within a few years had achieved an extremely high media profile. I followed the public affairs of the DCCBA with interest, especially their lively annual reports, which were always issued to the media with a view to publicity. Like all pressure groups, the DCCBA is particularly conscious of the need for publicity. I am a liberal and I found myself unable to share in many of the certainties of the DCCBA. On social issues I often found myself in disagreement with them and I made no secret of this.

Then something happened that was to put me and the DCCBA on a collision course. I have always had strong views about the conduct of the courts and the criminal justice system. As a young reporter I had spent a fair portion of my working life in the courts and I came to realise what a blessing a good system is and what horrors would await us if it ever failed to exist. So when I read in the association's annual review for 1988 such sentences as: "Crime clearly is not a by-product of poverty but of affluence..." and "The entire Irish system for crime prevention lacks an enterprise culture..." I felt that here, surely, was matter worthy of comment in Dubliner's Diary.

I found this paragraph on crime prevention particularly intriguing. It went on:

It must move towards some form of incentive system—rewarding prisons where fewer of their inmates re-offend, restructuring police and rewarding them only on the basis of local accountability and performance. Better management of the Police, Courts, Prisons, Revenue Collection and Schools is essential if crime-related costs are to be reduced for legitimate business.

Then followed a paragraph which said: "The independence of the judiciary is often quoted by those who wish to maintain the status quo and avoid necessary management changes in the criminal justice system. There is no conflict between an efficient criminal justice system and an independent judiciary; indeed, the quality of justice for victims would greatly benefit from a reformed, efficient, criminal justice system."

I found that statement disconcerting. I was aware—although the matter had attracted no publicity—that three years earlier the DCCBA had been involved in a bizarre incident with a member of the judiciary for which they were forced to make an out-of-court payment of £10,000 in settlement of the judge's suit for defamation. That incident involved Judge Gillian Hussey and her conduct of a district court case involving a street trader. On 15 August, 1985, Judge Hussey adjourned a case against a street trader pending the determination of a case stated to the High Court. This decision incensed the DCCBA, who now took steps to have their displeasure at the judge's decision made known to those who mattered.

The association wrote to the president of the district court, Judge Oliver Macklin, claiming that in her handling of the case Judge Hussey was not seen to be upholding the Gardaí and Dublin Corporation in their obligation to enforce the law, that she was acting as a social worker rather than a judge, and that her decision had been based on social attitudes rather than the law. Copies of the letter were then circulated by the association to, among others, the Minister for Justice and the Dublin city manager.

Judge Hussey consulted her solicitors, who demanded retraction of what they said was clear defamation and, by way of damages, payment of a sum to a charity of Judge Hussey's choice. The association replied that in the circumstances they would be prepared to make a payment to a charity but they wished to transmit the money themselves. This further infuriated the judge, who regarded this proviso as an extension of the initial defamation. On the advice of counsel, the DCCBA eventually handed over £10,000.

So when I came to comment on the report I decided to hone in on the question of the independence of the judiciary. My article was headed "The Hard Sell" and by any standards it was hard-hitting. "I'm sure there are some very intelligent people in the ranks of the Dublin City Centre Business Association," I wrote. "Well, its about time they started to cop themselves on. Every year when the annual report of the DCCBA is published we are treated to a treatise on law and order which would make the extreme wing of Margaret Thatcher's Conservative party blush...there is a telling final paragraph which says: 'Finally a word on the judiciary...'"

After quoting the relevant paragraph I added the comment: "We do, as it happens, have an independent judiciary in this country. It is one of the glories of our republic. God grant that our judges will never have to answer to the gentlemen of the Dublin City Centre Business Association and bow to their strange notions of justice."

I showed the DCCBA's letter to two legal friends, my solicitor, Colm Carville, and Sir James Comyn, a retired judge of the English high court, who was one of the leading libel experts at the English bar and who as a judge tried many notable libel cases, including that of the *Daily Mail v.* The Moonies, and Sidney Jameson *v.* the BBC. Jimmy Comyn's opening remark was most interesting and is, I think, a good example of how the legal mind works. "How does your editor feel about this, dear boy?" he asked. "What I mean is: if you were to have carried on in this appalling fashion for three whole years, surely your editor as the man charged with ensuring decent and proper standards in the newspaper must have acquiesced, for if he didn't acquiesce he must be grossly incompetent." That hadn't occurred to me—nor had it occurred to Sean Ward. It was, I thought, a most interesting point of view.

I had, of course, no problem in rebutting these astonishing and totally false charges. I was easily able to prove that far from being "persistently hostile to the business community in Dublin" I had in fact been supportive of it. It was also a simple matter to demolish the charge that I had written only "knocking copy" about the association or its prominent members over a period of three years.

I prepared a dossier of numerous cuttings from the diary supported by a dozen or so letters from prominent Dublin business people in which they expressed appreciation for fair and sympathetic coverage in Dubliner's Diary. The cuttings showed clearly that the charge of knocking copy could not be made to stand up. The letters included two signed by prominent members of the DCCBA, Arthur Walls, chief executive of Clery's, and Bill Kelly, marketing manager of Arnott's, who at that time was chairman of the DCCBA.

To this I added the entirely fair and objective profile of over 1,000 words which I had written on the DCCBA secretary, Tom Coffey, the man who signed the letter of complaint to Dr de Valera.

I then instructed Colm Carvill to send a rocket to the DCCBA calling for an immediate apology and retraction and the payment of a sum to charity. Failing that, I would sue for defamation. The DCCBA was in no mood to apologise. Back came an outraged letter from their solicitors claiming total justification and privilege and stating that any action brought by me would be vigorously defended and that there would be a counter suit for defamation against me as well!

After a further exchange of letters I knew it was a question of put up or shut up. I was not going to sue the DCCBA—to begin with I didn't have the financial resources and, secondly, I don't believe that journalists should have recourse to the libel courts except in the very gravest circumstances. There was, as it happened, another method of redress. To my surprise I discovered that Tom Coffey was a fully paid-up member of the NUJ. I initiated a disciplinary hearing under the NUJ's code of professional conduct; there was a preliminary hearing which decided that a prima-facie case had been made out and the matter then went to arbitration.

Eleven months after the complaint, Tom Coffey wrote again to Dr de Valera stating that the two allegations: (1) that I was persistently hostile to the business community and (2) that for three years I wrote only knocking copy about the DCCBA and its prominent members, were now unequivocally withdrawn and the association regretted that they had ever been made.

No one likes unfavourable let alone caustic comment and the business community is more intolerant of it than most. And, unlike most of the other recipients, the business community is in a position to impose sanctions. When the *Star* ran an article which the DCCBA regarded as unfairly critical of O'Connell Street and its Smurfit fountain it requested its members not to advertise in the newspaper.

The *Sunday Independent* lost a massive amount of advertising revenue after its exposé of the Irish Hospitals' Sweep in 1971...

And Harold Evans, as we have seen, was quite right in his fears about Distillers.

11

"PRAY FOR THE WANDERER"?

...the only people who don't appreciate how despised
they are are the journalists themselves.

Rev Martin Tierney, Director of the Catholic
Communications Institute of Ireland,
Catholic Herald and Standard, 15 August, 1991

All the power groupings in Irish society found it hard to
cope with the consequences of the media revolution of the
Sixties but none found it harder than the Roman Catholic
church. Of all the powerful institutions, the church proved
least able to cope with the new demands of TV and the
fresh approaches to news-gathering and comment that
quickly spread to the print media. The politicians and the
captains of industry soon became aware of what was
happening and flocked to experts such as Bunny Carr and
Mary Finan for guidance on how best they might cope
with the changes. The priests and the prelates—with a
couple of notable exceptions—resisted.

It is easy to see why they did. The institutional church
was, after all, the greatest propaganda machine the world

had ever known. In Catholic countries such as Ireland it enjoyed almost total monopoly of access. Every Sunday morning practically the entire adult population presented itself before its pulpits to receive instruction and indoctrination. In the schools thousands of devoted priests, nuns and religious brothers reiterated the church's message to the vast bulk of the nation's children. Those members of the laity—writers, journalists, broadcasters, members of the entertainment trades—who comprised what is now called the media were for the main part carefully controlled, censored and, if they stepped out of line, intimidated.

Many churchmen were as unprepared for the new order of things as was King Lear for the tempest. Their instinct was to flounder about in a fury, railing against the wrongness of it and behaving generally as if God had sent a messenger to say he had given up on them. Soon the sins of the media began to replace the sins of the flesh as the *bête noire* of the Roman Catholic church in Ireland. Just as thirty or forty years ago anathemas and threats of hell's torments were hurled at the fornicator and the masturbator, now it was errant journalists and media commentators who attracted the most doleful strictures of God's anointed.

"New Stalinists" recently ran the headline on yet another editorial condemning the media in the Redemptorist magazine *Reality*. The same magazine had earlier drawn a parallel between the tactics of the Irish media and those of the Nazis. "We don't want to be bulldozed and beaten by repeated claims that Irish marriage has broken down all round," wrote the editor, Rev KH Donlon CSsR, "that the situation is intolerable and that something must be done and what must be done is divorce. Those of us old enough to remember Hitler seem to remember that tactic before...It's the same tactic and the same deception..."

Week after week, the Catholic press lambasts what it contemptuously dismisses as "the secular media", frequently addressing its secular brothers on behalf of the nation. In the famous row over the alleged blasphemy by the *Irish Press* TV columnist Declan Lynch in August 1991 the *Irish Catholic*—even though it claims a circulation of no greater than 35,000—called upon the journalist and the paper to apologise "to the Irish people." In May 1984 *Reality* said: "Let us ask the media when they discuss divorce, to respect us, the people..."

Even the most venial transgressions of the secular media do not escape the strictures of the Catholic press. Under a headline "Disgraceful Journalism" the Dublin Diocesan Press Officer, Rev Tom Stack, admonished a named reporter of the *Irish Independent* for a number of solecisms in a funeral report, which included confusing the master of ceremonies with one of the concelebrants and styling the Abbot of Glenstal "Right Rev" instead of the affected and now widely disused appellation "Dom."

Those with even a smattering of church history are probably smiling cynically and asking what's new. The church, after all, has a notorious history of repression and persecution in regard to freedom of expression and communication. The theologian Hans Küng quotes a colleague on the topic of freedom and the church: "I know that there is freedom—but I didn't know that the church and freedom went together." Freedom of conscience and freedom of the press were still being condemned by popes until well into the nineteenth century, and the effects of the purge of scholars and intellectuals initiated by Pope Pius X (pope from 1903 to 1914) in his persecution of the "modernists" was still being felt fifty years after his death and involved even the young Angelo Roncalli, later Pope John XXIII. During the reign of Pope John Paul II numerous theologians, teachers and writers have been hounded out of office for departing from the official line and expressing the truths dictated by their consciences.

Attacks on journalists by Roman Catholic clerics have always been an occupational hazard in the newspaper business but this has become much more common since the emergence of the mass-circulation papers in the nineteenth century. A good example of the fear and paranoia of the media that existed in the Irish church at the turn of the last century can be found in a book called *The Young Priest's Keepsake* by the Rev Michael J Phelan SJ. Writing specifically for newly ordained priests back in 1904, Fr Phelan said:

> For the past 400 years the greatest evils that have afflicted the Church are traceable to a licentious press...Look at Europe today, seething with socialism and anarchy, its huge standing armies scarcely able to hold those worse than barbarian hordes in check. Out of what dark womb have these monsters crept? A corrupt press...The Reformation, the revolution, the social anarchy of today are the direct offspring of a licentious press...
>
> In proof of this we need look no further than our own

shores. Fifty years ago the priests of Ireland often had recourse to rough methods with the people. Even the aid of the blackthorn was occasionally invoked as an effective method of securing conviction. Yet, on the morrow, all was forgotten and the people would die for the man who had punished them.

Let the priest of today but thwart the grandchildren of that generation, even in a small matter, and mark the rancour...The spirit that Catholic Ireland had fifty years ago is sadly changed today and its tendency to fester on slight provocation is due to the poison instilled into it from an unwholesome anti-Catholic literature.

The wearisome rhetoric howls on, like wind through derelict tenements.

To journalists of my generation and previous ones incurring the displeasure of a powerful prelate could have serious consequences. Bill Sweetman, a former editor of the *Irish Press* and later a district-court judge, remembers a letter from the then president of Blackrock College and later Archbishop of Dublin, Dr John Charles McQuaid, seeking the removal of the sports editor because of a paragraph that did not do justice to the college rugby team. Poor old Maurice Liston, squirming with embarrassment and confusion as that same archbishop tore up the report he had respectfully submitted to him for vetting, would as a trade-union activist almost certainly have known about this and of the connection between Dr McQuaid and the de Valeras, and this knowledge would have concentrated his mind most powerfully in his response to the despotic and ignorant act.

Much bullying and intimidation went on behind the scenes. A good example of how things were done in the Fifties was the action initiated by the Bishop of Ossory and five of his senior clergy after a photograph of six women ballet dancers was published in the *Sunday Independent* on 1 May, 1955. On that Sunday the Independent published an article headed "Tóstal premiere for new Irish ballet" and the photograph of the six dancers was placed beside it. Five of the women wore leotards, the sixth was in modest black shorts and fishnet stockings. Four days after publication Bishop Patrick Collier and five of his senior clergy sent a letter to the editor of the *Sunday Independent*, Hector Legge.

They wished to inform him, they said, that they considered the photograph

a very unbecoming picture for a Sunday Catholic [*sic*] paper, a bad picture, dangerous for young and old. We take exception to a female figure almost nude in the group. Our considered opinion is that it may be classed as an objectionable picture...As readers of this paper, we consider we have a right to let you know what we consider wrong and as your customers we think you have an interest in knowing what readers think about what is served up to them in our papers, Sundays and weekdays. We want no publicity about this protest, we have not drawn public attention to it, we expect no explanation or defence. A word to your cameramen that your public do not want 'daring' or undressed groups or figures should be enough. We like decent pictures: the indecent we abhor as our religion demands. This is a private protest.

The editor was worried—as well he might be. He wrote to the Maynooth theologian and editor of *The Furrow*, Rev JJ McGarry. After making it clear that his comments were confidential and the assurance of a prayer to carry him over his editorial difficulties, Fr McGarry commented that the life of a Sunday newspaper editor was indeed a difficult one as he often found himself, as it were, "between the devil and the Holy See." The difficulty was, Fr McGarry felt, that there was

> an unenlightened element in Ireland, purely negative, focusing its spectacles to find something that will shock it. Ballet photographs are just the thing such people cannot understand...I cannot imagine how any charitable and understanding person could object to this photograph. Indeed I think the protest ridiculous...In the print I see the girl is actually wearing net stockings...I think that the journalist, and more especially the editor, must follow his conscience.

That was a daring suggestion in 1955—and probably explains why the theologian couldn't go public. It was, however, the bishop's view that held sway.

Although I never worked as a religious affairs correspondent, church-media relations have always been an area of prime interest to me. One day I propose to write a book on the subject and call it: *Days of Whines and Psychosis*. The unending stream of whinge, vituperation

and recrimination against the secular media has always—
as per Fr Phelan SJ—had a certain amusement value. But it
is basically very sad because it underlines what has to be
a very real dearth of faith in God's promise to his followers
that the gates of hell shall not prevail against them and it
alienates many good and sincere people in journalism and
in the church.

During my time as a features writer in the *Evening Press*
I often suggested articles about religious orders and their
members to coincide with special anniversaries or other
special occasions. In writing these articles neither I nor
the features editor Sean McCann ever harboured anything
other than sheer goodwill towards the subjects. Our aim
always was to show the positive side—and there always is
a positive side—and to help celebrate the occasion. Yet
practically every request was either refused or met with
paralysing suspicion. That I find very sad.

I can, of course, appreciate why it happens. Some of
these orders—the Irish Christian Brothers being the prime
example—have received extremely harsh media treatment
for past misdemeanours, real and imagined. The Irish
Christian Brothers are particularly unfortunate. As with the
city of Limerick it became something of a cult to rush into
print with yet another cautionary anecdote about a terrifying
past. The natural instinct when under attack like this is to
put the hands over the head and withdraw and it takes
courage to do the opposite. Yet I have seen one or two
moving and memorable TV pieces where members of that
order have spoken humbly and intelligently about these
difficulties and where the media treatment was sensitive

and unsmarmy.

Many priests and prelates who should know better like to spread the notion that there is some sort of plot against the Roman Catholic church in the Irish media. They talk of the media as if it were some alien monolith imposed upon Ireland from outer space. There is no plot. And this fearful monolith which they dread is comprised of their own brothers and sisters, cousins, neighbours. The great conflict between the two sides arises because a large proportion of those who work in the media are liberals and, though the majority of them are practising Roman Catholics, they generally refuse to act as propagandists for the church nor will they accept without question the rampant authoritarianism which still flourishes within it.

Life was so much easier before nineteen sixty-three when, according to Philip Larkin, sexual intercourse began

> Between the end of the Chatterley ban
> And the Beatles' first LP.

The combined shockwaves of Vatican II and the coming of television took some time to have their effect. Then the rumblings started. Soon it was obvious that many churchmen were fearful and angry. Bishop Brendan Comiskey, then an assistant bishop in Dublin, observed on a number of occasions that "the magisterium was moving from Maynooth to Montrose" and he frequently quoted Anthony Smith's assertion that "the media somewhere towards the middle of the 1960s in most western countries, decided that their historic role was to confront and expose."

Bishop Comiskey was seen by many of his fellow clergy as a man who wasn't afraid to fire a few shots across the bows of the newly fortified media. He gave new heart to many churchmen who rallied to him in his battle against what had now come to be perceived as the biggest single obstacle to the advancement of the church in Ireland. An accomplished TV performer and a prolific writer, he was the first member of the Irish hierarchy to be drawn from outside the ranks of the secular clergy since the appointment of John Charles McQuaid in 1940. Born in Clontibret, Co Monaghan, one of a family of ten, he joined the missionary congregation of the Sacred Hearts of Jesus and Mary and went to the US for part of his clerical training. By the time he was thirty-five he had served a term as provincial superior of his congregation and at forty-four he was the youngest bishop in Ireland.

Since his appointment Bishop Comiskey has kept a high media profile and has rarely been out of the headlines. Even though I believe his media criticism to be chiefly propagandist and sometimes unfair, journalists owe him a big debt of gratitude. More than any other person he forced debate on the media at a time when there was little enthusiasm for it. In doing so he focused on two of the deadly sins of the Irish media—its reluctance to look objectively on its own activities and its almost total inability to report objectively on the media industry. The bishop hasn't had a great deal of success in forcing reformation on these points, but his appetite for the fray and his enthusiasm for the correction of the media in general have remained so keen that he must now carry the most dinted crozier in

Christendom.

In July 1991 he clashed with the *Irish Press* in what was to my mind one of the most unfortunate episodes in church-media relations in decades. Possibly because of the *Irish Press* management's strenuous and commercially sensible efforts at damage limitation it received relatively little publicity. It was, I believe, an occasion in which the bishop acted unfairly against a vulnerable newspaper and the 550 people employed in it.

In what was to become known as the *Irish Press* blasphemy case, the paper's freelance TV critic, Declan Lynch, said in one of his columns that, "Hopefully if the singing Madonna ever has a son he will give less trouble than the precocious Nazarene." As I read Declan's piece that Saturday morning I said to myself, "There's a cheap shot that should never have got into the paper." If I had been editing the column I wouldn't have let it stand.

Not that the word blasphemy had even entered my head. I'm always loath to apply the term to any piece of writing as I have no way of knowing whether the deity considers it blasphemous and that, after all, must remain the real test. On balance my instinct tells me that God, if indeed there is a God, doesn't much mind what is said about him or her in the TV column of the *Irish Press* of a Saturday morning. I tend to side with Swift, who on the separate but in its time also thorny question of Friday abstinence wrote:

> Does any man of common sense
> Think ham and eggs gives God offence?

Or that the herring has a charm
The almighty's anger to disarm?
Wrapped in his majesty divine
Do you think he cares on what we dine?

But that's not the point. I like to think that God may have a sense of humour, although I concede that this notion may be repugnant theologically. The more pressing point is that while it is possible that God may not be in the least bit offended, there could be no doubt whatever that many good, sincere and decent people here on earth were, for a variety of reasons, certain to be scandalised, outraged and offended on God's behalf. An unspecified number of these good people contacted Bishop Comiskey after reading the article that Saturday morning and the following week the bishop turned his *Irish Catholic* column into "An Open Letter to the *Irish Press*."

In the hallowed traditions of those correspondents who begin their complaints with the line "My attention has been drawn..." (euphemism for "You don't think I'd buy your wretched rag"), Bishop Comiskey (though not in that clichéd phrase) informed us that he does not take the *Irish Press*. I was taken aback by the admission that he was not a regular reader as I had assumed that all members of the hierarchy (let alone one of its principal media experts) would as a matter of course at least scan all the national papers daily.

The bishop started his column with what is known in the trade as a slow burner—a technique designed to heighten the impact of the main point when it finally emerges. It took him eleven paragraphs to get to the main point: "If we take the definition of blasphemy given by the *Oxford English Dictionary*, 'profane speaking of God and sacred things,' then Mr Lynch and the *Irish Press* are blasphemers."

After a reference to the paper's motto, "Do chum glóire Dé agus onóra na hÉireann," Bishop Comiskey declared that not only was the piece blasphemous before God, but also deeply offensive to all who believe that Jesus Christ is the Son of God.

"How far the *Irish Press* has fallen," he added, "from the days when it was founded to champion the culture, the aspirations, and the values of the Irish people. Last week it reached a new low. It is one thing to be anti-clerical and to adopt an anti-Catholic Church line. Church-bashing is one thing. Blasphemy is something else."

Having dealt with the spiritual aspects of the case, the bishop now speedily moved to the temporal. "I have advised those who have asked my advice," he wrote, "to write to the *Irish Press* and to express their views as strongly as they expressed them to me. The more radical response, of course, is to withdraw one's support from the paper by ceasing to purchase it or to advertise in it."

The bishop didn't use the word boycott—indeed it may never have entered his mind. But it was the word that entered the minds of many of the 550 employees of Irish Press Newspapers whose jobs had already been on the line for longer than most of them cared to remember. Even though he was not a regular reader, Bishop Comiskey could scarcely be unaware of the precarious future of Irish Press

Newspapers.

Three points struck me immediately about Bishop Comiskey's open letter:

(1): If this incident represented a "new low" then, logically, there must have been previous lows. The bishop didn't identify them.

(2): "It is one thing to be anti-clerical and to adopt an anti-Catholic Church line." The *Irish Press* was, therefore, anti-clerical and anti-Catholic church. But these charges were unsubstantiated.

(3): "Church-bashing is one thing. Blasphemy is something else..." The *Irish Press*, therefore, was a paper that engaged in church-bashing. But again, the charges were unsubstantiated.

These innuendos were simply outrageous. The *Irish Press* was never—then or previously—anti-clerical. The *Irish Press* never engaged in church-bashing, nor did it have an anti-church line. How Bishop Comiskey could come to make these charges is beyond me.

Vincent Jennings, the then *Irish Press* chief executive, was at the time of Bishop Comiskey's attack the chairman of Veritas, the Roman Catholic publishing concern. As long as I had worked with him—which is over twenty-five years—I had never known him to be other than punctilious in insisting in fairness for all parties written about in the newspapers. If the *Irish Press* had been indulging in church-bashing, then he, as chief executive and deputy editor-in-chief, and Éamon de Valera, as chairman and editor-in-chief, would, between them, have had to countenance it. To anyone who knows these men, the idea would be preposterous. None of the three editors I have known and worked with over the past twenty years, would have allowed any member of their staff to engage in church-bashing.

The *Irish Press* did as the *Irish Catholic* (speaking editorially) commanded it to do—it apologised, not "to the Irish people" on whose behalf the *Irish Catholic* was doing the ordering but to those readers who had been offended. About sixty people wrote in complaining, many stating that they would no longer buy the paper or advertise in it.

While some attempts, scholarly and otherwise, have been made to analyse the church-media impasse and to try and discover the root cause of the acrimony, the point-scoring and the suspicion that all too often characterises an encounter between both sides, little progress has been made. This isn't surprising for until recent years little or no academic research was carried out on the Irish media.

The bulk of the blame lies with the media themselves: with newspapers, that want to analyse and pontificate on every industry in the country yet shy away from any analysis of their own affairs; with the NUJ, which has a sweet tooth for bizarre political dogma the propagation of which has caused widespread confusion regarding the objectivity of journalists, and with the journalists themselves, who tend to be notoriously apathetic when it comes to developing their own profession and projecting a proper image of it. The insistence of some branches of the NUJ in issuing policy statements on matters such as abortion, the Gulf War and other social issues has given an ideal opportunity to unscrupulous critics of the media who suggest—quite wrongly—that these policy statements are binding on the members.

One of the better contributions to the church-media debate is an essay "The Church and the Press: Living with Liberalism" written by Andy Pollak, religious affairs correspondent of *The Irish Times* and published in *The Furrow*. He wrote that when he moved to *The Irish Times* from Belfast five years previously one thing that quickly struck him was the atmosphere in Dublin newsrooms.

It was liberal, sceptical, slightly iconoclastic, careless of reputation, concerned about journalistic independence and accuracy, and congenitally anxious to ferret out the truth about the powerful, the secretive, the unaccountable...

It is the first of these epithets I believe is the key to understanding the inevitable tension between a hierarchic Church and the Press in a democratic society: the essential liberalism of the journalistic profession, a liberalism which makes many bishops and priests feel distinctly uneasy nearly 130 years after Pius IX's condemnation of it in the Syllabus of Errors.

Even the most politically and theologically conservative journalist has to become a liberal when at work. Without freedom of conscience, opinion and expression and as free a flow of ideas as a society of powerful vested interests allows, the job of informing people about the events that shape their lives would be impossible. In this sense I often think it must be much easier to come to journalism from a background of Protestantism or liberal democracy, with the emphasis on the primacy of the individual and his or her conscience, rather than Roman Catholicism or Marxist centralism with their implicit or explicit stress on truth as interpreted and handed down by an unaccountable magisterium...

That, I believe, is true. And so, I believe, is Dr Tom Inglis's assessment in his book *Moral Monopoly: The Catholic Church in Modern Irish Society*.

If the power of the Catholic Church in Ireland has begun to dwindle in recent years it is not so much that it can no longer limit other power blocs and alliances, but that its control of moral practice and discourse is being eroded by the development of mass communications. The media have lifted the veil of silence which previously shrouded moral issues...

It is the media that have shattered the myth that it is bad luck to criticise the priest. It is the media that have broken the tradition of not criticising the Church and its teachings in public. It is the media that have forced the Church into giving a public account of itself. It was the media, and particularly television, which brought to an end the long nineteenth-century tradition of Irish Catholicism...

12

UP IN THE AIR

Lovers of air travel find it exhilarating to hang poised between the illusion of immortality and the fact of death.

Alexander Chase

Campari and soda in hand, the great John Cecil Kelly-Rogers, Captain, Officer of the Order of the British Empire, Fellow of the Royal Aeronautical Society, Liveryman of the Guild of Air Pilots and Navigators, was in expansive mood. Aer Lingus, he volunteered, was the natural consequence of a merger between the peasantry and high technology. I could see what he was getting at. JCKR, as he was known in Aer Lingus, had spent most of his career with Imperial Airways and the British Overseas Airways Corporation. He had flown Sir Winston Churchill on important wartime missions. He was imperious and irreverent but it was the irreverent side of him that sparked the remark about Aer Lingus.

He was coming to the end of his most distinguished career when, towards the close of the Sixties, I got to know him slightly. He came to Aer Lingus in 1947 but his flying career had ended with the seaplanes and he now worked as a senior executive. Kelly-Rogers put his stamp on the fledgeling Aer Lingus in several ways. He felt that the pilots should salute the executives when they met on the tarmac or around the airport. The Aer Lingus pilots, who, like most airline pilots, must have harboured at least a slight degree of contempt for mere groundlings, would have none of it. A proposal then came from management that the pilots should undergo routine psychiatric checks. The pilots said that was fine with them provided the management underwent similar testing. The idea was dropped.

No other professional group has done a finer public-relations job on itself in so short a time as have airline pilots. Like surgeons, they have a great leverage on the public imagination. If the plumber or the chef or the accountant lets you down you may be drenched, starved or broke in that order. If the pilot or the surgeon lets you down you will almost certainly be maimed or killed. That is why people like to look up to surgeons and airline pilots even though there is plenty of evidence to show that they are as human as the rest of us. But we and they need a proper sense of perspective. None of us should be too astonished that the descendants of the people who built Newgrange, produced the Book of Kells and wrote *Ulysses* should in time come to master the intricacies of the DC-3.

Captain Darby Kennedy, doyen of Irish flying instructors and one of Ireland's most distinguished pilots, is on record as saying that, given the time, he could teach a monkey to fly. And, by way of proving that, he taught me. I am an aviation buff. Ever since I saw my first airplane—a magnificent Lockheed Constellation L-049 in the silver and blue livery of Pan American World Airways—"The System of the Flying Clippers"—aviation has been one of my great loves. Like Alexander Chase, I have always found flying exhilarating even if I have never associated it with death. I've never had even a remote fear of flying and anyway the safety statistics should convince even the most nervous.

I will always be grateful to the *Irish Press* for giving me the opportunity of covering aviation as their air correspondent. Few news reporters are lucky enough to be able to work at their hobby—a privilege which many of our colleagues in the sports department enjoy. My friend Karl Johnston, for example, is lucky enough to be able to devote all his working life to his twin passions of rugby and cricket as the rugby and cricket correspondent of the *Irish Press*. Unfortunately, no national newspaper in Ireland has ever had a full-time aviation correspondent. And thereby hangs a tale, because if the industry is to be thoroughly reported and analysed it would at the very least require the attentions of a full-time correspondent. And the industry would be all the better as a consequence.

Aviation—and in particular national airlines—is the very stuff of which propaganda is made. For this reason alone it should be carefully monitored and reported on by specialists who have the time and resources to meet head on the propaganda that airlines, like all powerful institutions, use as oxygen.

This propaganda is never more strident than when state airlines start feeding off national pride. And has there ever been an emergent nation that didn't feel compelled to establish a great flag-carrier airline to show the world that it had come of age as a nation?

Michael Dargan—the most forceful of all Aer Lingus chief executives and a man with a taste for rhetoric—knew the value of national pride in bolstering the image of an airline. Soon after taking office he summoned an international aviation conference in Dublin and proceeded to play the nationalist card as expertly as any politician. "We have honoured the trust of our small country," he said, "by demonstrating that we could match the world in one of its most sophisticated industries and in this we have contributed to the confidence of our young generation in Ireland."

Rousing stuff. It is, of course, absolutely true that Aer Lingus in its foundation and development had contributed to the confidence of successive generations in Ireland. But to suggest that Ireland could match the world with its Pan Ams, its Aeroflots, its Boeings and its McDonnell Douglases was, even allowing for national fervour, stretching things a bit. By the time I came to cover aviation in the 1960s Aer Lingus had already built up a very effective propaganda machine. In 1936, when it was founded, state intervention in industry often met with great political opposition and there was an obvious need to convince the public and— even more importantly—the legislature that a state-owned national airline was an essential instrument of a modern nation.

At the beginning, under JF Dempsey, Aer Lingus propaganda seemed to centre on three things: reliability, smallness and holiness. Then, with the arrival of Michael

J Dargan, the emphasis swung to aggressiveness and independence. David Kennedy's term of office was marked by a softening of the image and Aer Lingus became the thinking man's airline. Cathal Mullen's hallmark seems to be no-nonsense pragmatism with flashes of Darganesque militancy.

I have long been fascinated by the role of religion in Aer Lingus propaganda. I'm not suggesting that religious traditions or customs were ever cynically used for commercial advantage, but Joyce's assertion that in Ireland Christ and Caesar were hand in glove was certainly true of Aer Lingus.

All Aer Lingus aircraft were (and still are) named after saints. In the early days the airplanes were blessed every year in a ceremony on the ramp at Dublin Airport. Aircraft that were out on service were deemed to have been blessed *in absentia*. I remember being in the circuit in a light aircraft on one of these occasions and hearing an SAS pilot demand to know why he was being delayed in getting permission to start his engines. The controller briefly explained about the blessing ceremony and requested patience. "And when I am late in Copenhagen I can tell them you were all saying your prayers at Dublin Airport?" the SAS man replied cynically.

Aer Lingus has always—and rightly—put great emphasis on presenting a good public image. In the early days that was no easy task. The supposed worldwide perception of Irishmen as wild feckless belligerent creatures who would sell their sisters into white slavery for drink money was not a particularly good base on which to build a pilot and technical corps. Yet from the earliest years of aviation Irishmen (and, increasingly, Irishwomen) have excelled in the aviation industry. Our geographic location thrust us into the mainstream of aviation activity during the very early days. Ireland now has a fine aviation tradition and Irish pilots, engineers, and air traffic controllers are as technically skilled as any in the world. But as I say—this shouldn't be the cause of great wonderment. We Irish are a very intelligent people.

The great father figure of Aer Lingus, Jeremiah F Dempsey, was still in the driving seat when I started working as an air correspondent. The airline and indeed the country owes him a great deal. A man of fearsome integrity, he initiated the "canvassing will disqualify" code for job applicants in Aer Lingus. I remember him telling me that he had a big problem convincing people that it actually meant what it said.

"I developed a formula for dealing with any politician, business contact or acquaintance who might phone me up about a candidate," he said. "I'd listen patiently to the preliminary spiel. Then just as they were starting on the excellent qualities of their client I'd say: 'Breathe not the name.' That was usually met with an incredulous 'Are you really serious?' and I'd say 'Of course we are serious—did you not see the advertisement?'"

During that first year (1936) he would see off the plywood and canvas bi-plane every day. Sometimes when there were no passengers he would insist that it went anyway. "We were based in Baldonnel and the airplane would fly over O'Connell Street on the way to the coast.

Everyone would look up when it passed over and if it didn't come the word would go round. I was determined to build up a reputation for punctuality and it was worth sending it for that alone."

The pride which the Irish people had in the early Aer Lingus is borne out by a confidential 1953 memorandum from the British Commonwealth Office to the Ministry of Civil Aviation and released under the thirty-year rule. "Our ambassador in Dublin," the memorandum states, "has pointed out that, politically, it must be borne in mind that Aer Lingus is the pride and joy of the average Irishman...He looks on it as a striking example of Irish achievement and efficiency—something that has put the republic back on the map of the world after long years of wartime isolation..."

There was a legend propagated by the Aer Lingus press office which claimed that at the start the airline's complete set of spares were kept in a biscuit tin. JF Dempsey's successor, Michael J Dargan, had no time for biscuit tins. A doughty former civil servant, Dargan was one of those who believed that had Aer Lingus been allowed to go ahead with its planned North Atlantic service in 1948, Ireland would now have an airline spanning the entire globe. When he took over in 1968 he spoke in terms of supersonic transports carrying the Irish flag across the Atlantic and six-lane highways linking Dublin Airport with the city centre. (The supersonic transports, on two of which Aer Lingus had options, were never built. The six-lane highway did materialise—twenty years later.)

Dargan thought big, talked tough and suffered fools not at all. He fought hard to try and loosen the grip of the civil service on the airline and with the chief press officer, Captain Jack Millar, he conducted a brilliant propaganda campaign in an effort to keep American airlines out of Dublin Airport. He once berated me because of what he claimed was the media's fondness for producing weather stories which led potential tourists to believe that the Irish climate was unpleasant. The fact that we were at that very moment sitting in an Aer Lingus Viscount which was circling Cork Airport in the hope that the foul weather would lift and allow us to land did not, to his mind, weaken his argument in the slightest. Jack Millar is a Strabane man. He came to Aer Lingus from the (Irish) army which was the basis for his frequent boast: "There are nearly two hundred captains in this shagging company and I'm the only genuine one." Intensely loyal to Aer Lingus and to its management, he could be combative when he felt the interests of his beloved airline were being threatened. I liked him a lot and despite many a row over some silly "emergency" or some real or imaginary slight in which, perhaps, IATA (International Air Transport Association) was described as a cartel or Aer Lingus was said to be in receipt of a subsidy, we were and have remained good friends.

"Cartel" and "subsidy" were two words which rated as gross obscenities in the Aer Lingus lexicon of that period. At the mention of the word "subsidy" Michael Dargan's face would darken and all eyes would turn on him in anticipation of the inevitable thunder clap. It used be said that Jack Millar—a considerable stylist—had worn out several dictionaries of synonyms and antonyms in his efforts to coin suitable euphemisms for these two words so that the Aer Lingus annual report and the frequent press releases would not be fouled by them. In the end it scarcely mattered. Time changes everything and eventually it even put manners on IATA. There are very few nowadays who would defend the price-fixing activities of that imperious trade union of the airlines and it would be a brave accountant who would claim that capital freely given without expectation of a dividend is other than a hidden subsidy.

And, of course, for years Aer Lingus freely entered into a cartel arrangement with several other state airlines, most notoriously the Netherlands carrier KLM, to whom they paid a large annual sum to prevent their competing on the Dublin-Amsterdam route.

On the Dublin-London service (the second busiest air route in Europe and once one of the most lucrative) there was a long-standing cartel arrangement with British Airways. Both airlines fixed the fares, frequencies and standard of service and, at the end of the day, split the profits. Another big propaganda war was fought on this issue. Aer Lingus reacted vigorously—far too vigorously—to the first faint stirrings of consumerism in the late Sixties and early Seventies. The thinking seemed to be that if you shout loud and long enough at the protesters you will intimidate them and they will go away.

Maeve Binchy was then the extremely well-informed tourism correspondent of *The Irish Times* and she was frequently in the thick of these rows. Another area of conflict on which Maeve had superb inside information was the strange relationship between Aer Lingus and Bord Fáilte.

There was astonishing antipathy between these bodies, particularly with regard to the US routes. Aer Lingus pursued a relentless and self-centred campaign to promote its own interest while Bord Fáilte naturally had to look to increasing the number of tourists irrespective of who flew them. Both companies found that they had to walk tightropes. Bord Fáilte could not be seen to be knocking the national airline or doing anything to jeopardise the Shannon stopover. The Aer Lingus people had to be careful not to let any falling-off in service occur to prevent any accusations that they were slowing down the tourist industry for their own selfish ends. Both sides had to be careful not to fall foul of the minister.

Maeve could charm a story out of the most sullen and unwilling of subjects—indeed I believe she could charm anything out of anyone. Once when we were in London working on some story or other we went to Park Lane to inspect the newly opened Hilton and its much-talked-about roof bar. Installed at the counter and seeking refreshment, Maeve was told by a very starchy barman that we would have to move as it was not customary to serve ladies at the bar. Maeve gave him a sweet smile and said: "Take a good long look at me, love. Now do I look even remotely like a lady?" We got the gin and tonics.

Just as Queen Mary could not bear to see her husband George V's obituary appear first in the evening papers and so allowed the king's physician to help him on his way so that he made the first edition of *The Times*, so Jack Millar for years did his utmost to keep the Aer Lingus annual report for the morning papers. As the press conference was always held at 3 pm we felt we should have access but Jack just kept saying "Och, noo, noo, noo" to all our pleadings and embargoed the thing until six. Great games were played and great strategies were employed by us to get hold of a copy and on a few occasions we succeeded.

In the Sixties there was a tendency for newspapers to exaggerate or, as we say in the trade, "flam up," minor incidents involving airplanes. An airplane turning back after an engine failure is normally a very minor thing with little or no risk attached for either passengers or crew. These were sometimes turned into events of high drama and the airlines—all of whom are intensely sensitive in regard to all safety matters—frequently and justifiably complained that nervous passengers as well as the relatives of those involved were being unduly distressed because of this unprofessional conduct.

I had no difficulty in agreeing with most of this. I believe that the travelling public has the right to know about engine failures, slight as the risk may be. But the reports should be brief and responsibly done. Unfortunately since most reporters are incapable of distinguishing an aileron from an elevator, and as most eyewitnesses and participants in these events give either exaggerated or totally cockeyed accounts of them, there is plenty of scope for misrepresentation.

My views on these matters happened to coincide with those of Sean Ward, then the group chief news editor, and between us we worked to ensure that coverage of air incidents, accidents and disasters would be responsible and as accurate as we could possibly make it. And in this, I believe, we succeeded.

Then Aer Lingus lost a Viscount in a heavy landing in Bristol and I learned that the industry is every bit as prone to irresponsible conduct in these matters as are the media.

As there were no available scheduled flights to Bristol that day I chartered a light aircraft and arrived just on the deadline for the final edition. On final approach I could see the Viscount, the shamrock and the Aer Lingus markings already painted over, and it appeared that its back was broken. On the ground I soon found an official. With only minutes to get the story over I wanted answers to two questions: Had there been injuries and was the aircraft a write-off? I was told there were no injuries and that the aircraft would soon be serviceable again. I took both answers in good faith and filed my story accordingly. When I got back there was a lot of explaining to do to WJR. The aircraft's back was indeed broken and it was a write-off, and two people had been taken to hospital—admittedly with minor injuries but injuries nevertheless.

Years later when the Douglas DC-10 airplane was going through a period of protracted difficulties, Aer Lingus leaked to the media biased technical information which suggested that the model was unsafe. When the battle of the North Atlantic hotted up and Aer Lingus was under the direst pressure from Transamerica, a US airline long since defunct, it circulated selective information which, taken in isolation, would lead to the quite erroneous conclusion that Transamerica was an irresponsible airline.

Practically every air crash unfurls an almost unbearable tapestry of human suffering: broken bodies lying in makeshift morgues; numbed relatives and friends walking aimlessly about; rescue workers feigning detached professionalism when, more often than not, they are on the point of breaking down. They too are especially difficult to report. If officialdom had its way there would be no coverage of crashes at all—as indeed was the case in the USSR until very recently. In addition to the human tragedy there are often huge vested interests involved. Airlines, aircraft manufacturers, civil aviation authorities and trade unions have all at one time or another been guilty of trying to arrange cover-ups or to shift the blame from where it belongs.

There have been several appalling air disasters in Ireland, mainly in the Shannon area and most of them long forgotten. But the crash of the Aer Lingus Viscount St Phelim near Tuskar Rock off the Wexford coast in March 1968 was to become one of the most talked-about and written-about crashes in the history of civil aviation.

I spent nearly three months in Wexford during that spring and summer as hopes faded for the recovery of all but a few of the bodies and as Royal Navy divers dragged the seabed in the hope of finding the wreckage and discovering some clue as to what had sent sixty-one people to their deaths on that bright March Sunday morning. If ever a crash called for sensitive handling it was this one. Added to the torment of the bereaved were the weeks of waiting in the hope that more bodies would be found. For most of the relatives that wait ended in the trusting and accepting words of the service of burial at sea: "We therefore commit their bodies to the deep...looking for the resurrection of the body (when the sea shall give up her dead)..."

There was some irresponsible and insensitive reporting—and from some unexpected quarters—of the finding of bodies that had not in fact been found. That, I accept, is inexcusable. But communications with officialdom were appalling, and when that situation occurs irresponsible reporting is more or less inevitable. It shouldn't happen but it almost invariably does.

We have come some way since the Sixties when the view of most civil servants was that reporters, and the public whom they represented, should be fobbed off with the bare minimum of information or, if possible, with no information at all. In the case of air disasters this attitude led to anger, frustration and, ultimately, paranoia. In the absence of solid information rumours abound and some of these inevitably find their way into the news pages. Then even the most responsible reporters find themselves on the defensive, explaining to their news editors how the story printed by a rival isn't exactly true.

Twenty years after the Tuskar Rock crash the Department of Transport inspector in charge of the investigation, RW O'Sullivan, published his memoirs and I was astounded to find in them an allegation of phone-tapping by reporters covering the crash. "The investigation was not helped," he wrote, "by interference caused by the tapping of telephone lines to such an extent that a scrambler had to be introduced between the office of the inspector of accidents and all outside lines. This action had to be taken to minimise the leakage of information of confidential matters and discussions covering instructions to inspectors in the field which were being reported in a distorted fashion in the newspapers."

As I had no memory of these distorted reports I arranged to interview Mr O'Sullivan in the hope that he might substantiate or amplify this most fascinating allegation. However, he was very vague about the whole business and couldn't provide any concrete evidence.

My own recollection of the telephone facilities in the Harbour View Hotel (where the investigation team and most of the media were based) was that they were very primitive—so much so that they might have come off the set of *The Quiet Man*. There were no telephones in the rooms but as a concession to newspaper reporters an extra line was installed in a corridor where after cranking a handle you could bypass the Rosslare operator and get through to Wexford. The morning after it was installed a honeymoon couple, believing it to be the link with room service, cranked the handle and informed the Wexford operator that they wanted one orange juice, one half-grapefruit, two bacon-and-eggs and two tea-and-toasts sent up to room seven. The operator dutifully recorded the order and phoned it back to Mrs Griffin, who had the breakfasts sent up.

As Mr O'Sullivan says in his book, there has been much ignorant speculation as to what happened to the Viscount. That makes his own theory all the more valuable. He says that while the cause of the accident could not be positively established, "there is quite strong circumstantial evidence that another aircraft or flying vehicle (manned or unmanned) was in the vicinity and resulted either in a positive collision, for which no physical evidence was discovered but which cannot be excluded, or a very near miss which caused an 'upset' resulting in a violent manoeuvre of the Viscount. I incline towards this as being probably the most likely case..."

If Mr O'Sullivan's theory is correct—and he is a highly experienced and respected aviation expert—then it is virtually certain that officialdom—in this case the British government or perhaps NATO—lied and lied and lied about the cause of the Viscount disaster.

Throughout the Seventies and Eighties there was a build-up of haughtiness, even arrogance in Aer Lingus. Successive generations of Aer Lingus staff had come up through a culture of monopoly and protectionism. In the collective subconscious of Aer Lingus was the deeply rooted belief that the bottomless purse of the exchequer would always be there to see them through their difficulties. Restrictive practices were rampant and in some cases staff had grown accustomed to thinking first of their own comfort and convenience and putting the passengers second.

There were serious difficulties in the hostess corps and these were highlighted in the PhD thesis of Geraldine O'Brien, an executive in the personnel department, part of which was published in *IBAR*, a journal of the Institute of Public Administration. This revealed many restrictive practices and trade-union militancy which were causing real inconvenience to passengers, often to the point of having flights delayed and even cancelled. It was strong stuff: members of the senior management were quoted and there could be no doubt in anyone's mind but that the situation was drastic.

I wrote a piece based on the *IBAR* article which I felt would make an interesting "bottom-of-the-page" item for page one. But it so happened that there was no news of any consequence that day and my piece, nicely garnished with banner headlines, ended up as the lead story. There was great fury in Aer Lingus. All the hoary old shibboleths were trotted out: sensational reporting...gross exaggeration... taken out of context...As Brendan Behan used to say: "You could sing it if you had an air to it!"

Within a couple of years the propaganda war had been lost, the cartel broken and Aer Lingus changed almost beyond recognition. The joint catalysts were a grocer's daughter from Grantham and an engine-driver's son from Thurles. Margaret Thatcher had almost single-handedly created the commercial environment in which Tony Ryan could openly challenge his former employers. Mr Ryan likes to maintain the fiction that he has little or nothing to do with the airline that bears the family name. His sons are listed as the principal proprietors and he brought in Arthur Walls, a doughty heavyweight of the aviation industry and a former deputy general manager of Aer Lingus, to front the operation as its chairman.

The loophole was Luton. The cartel controlled the rights to the two established airports for London, Heathrow and Gatwick. Ryanair sought rights to Luton and the then Minister for Transport, Jim Mitchell, gave the go-ahead. Nothing would ever be quite the same again. I travelled on the inaugural flight in the old and noisy BAC 748 twin-prop. At the airport Arthur Walls was snubbed by several of his former colleagues. A Jesuit from Clongowes Wood College came and blessed the old 748. I had never been to Luton before and I wasn't impressed. I came to the conclusion that the new venture had only a very limited chance of success.

I was wrong. Although Ryanair (in common with practically every other airline in the world) was to run into almost insurmountable difficulties during the recession of 1990-1, the Luton venture proved to be an idea in perfect harmony with the mood of the moment. Aided by a very clever advertising and PR campaign, it fired the imagination of a public that was sick and tired of monopolies and nicely indoctrinated in the virtues of private enterprise. With media and public alike, the infant Ryanair became the darling of the hour.

At first Aer Lingus more or less ignored it. Soon it became obvious that not only would Ryanair not go away but it was fast becoming a real commercial threat. This isn't the place in which to detail the brutal and bloody encounters that ensued—battles that were intensified by the arrival on the Dublin-Heathrow route of British Midland Airways, which promptly offered a club-class service for everyone.

The initial successes of Ryanair helped Aer Lingus management not only severely to dint the stranglehold of restrictive practices that existed but to introduce work practices which would have been laughed out of court by the trade unions a couple of years earlier. There are three major partners in every airline—the consumer, the proprietor and the worker. Now at last the advantage was swinging towards the consumer.

Ryanair was modelled on the start-up airlines that sprang into existence by the dozen in the US following President Carter's deregulation of the airlines. The emphasis was on a young, eager, non-union staff; a minimum of fixed assets; a small but aggressive management team; and oceans of PR and advertising hype which emphasised the freshness of youth and the glories of the free market.

The notion of the sanctity of the free market took a bashing when Ryanair, after a year of heavy losses, went knocking on the door of the Transport Minister, Seamus Brennan, seeking the self-same commercial advantage which they recently held in such contempt. It must have been particularly galling for Aer Lingus to be forced by Mr Brennan to abandon three of their routes in favour of the troubled Ryanair.

Aviation has always greatly interested me as a journalist and if my fairy godmother came and said I could have any job I wished in newspapers I would elect to be a full-time aviation correspondent. Perhaps this interest goes back to my catering days in Shannon, when life seemed so full of promise and the romance of the big lumbering piston engine airliners, the Constellations, the Stratocruisers and the DC-7s, was still a daily reality. In the Fifties Shannon (or "the base," as the locals in Rineanna always called it) was still the undisputed link between two civilisations. Then an Atlantic crossing was still both an adventure and an ordeal and to watch a great airliner come in over the estuary after what would now be regarded as an eternity over the ocean was always a thrill to me.

In those days the eastbound airliners arrived early in

the morning and there would be joyous scenes as elder brothers and sisters, gaudily jewelled and clad in mauves and yellow ochres, hugged blushing siblings and tearful fathers and mothers saying: "Gee...but you folks look great." And in the evenings, when the clippers and the Constellations were being fuelled for the journey west, others would come but there would be no loud clothes and no whoops of joy or surprise. And in each of these pathetic groups one or sometimes two or even three youngsters would carry under their arms the big envelope containing the chest X-ray that would prove to the medical officer of the port authority of New York or Chicago or Boston that they were free of tuberculosis.

Sometimes a parent or an uncle who might be flush would bring them to the public restaurant, where they would sit silently and uncomfortably gazing at the menu. The uncle or the father might attempt a joke—usually a line to say they shouldn't be afraid to order something grand as the menu said this was Shannon *Free* Airport. And even though their hearts were breaking they would all laugh and ask either for a "meat tea" or a "plain tea." And so the cycle, the accursed, vicious cycle of emigration, went on. And not always without humour. I remember one morning when a newly fledged Yank, a young woman of astonishing brashness with two cameras (cine and box Brownie), a sequined hat and even more bangles than usual, trooped into the restaurant followed by her mortified family and addressed herself loudly to Ted Deegan, the long-suffering headwaiter.

"Do you have cawfie here," she drawled.

Ted responded with another question: "Did we have it the night you were going out?"

POSTSCRIPT

(The time so short, the craft so hard to learn...)

So there it is, my first thirty years in journalism. Sometimes it seems incredible that three decades have passed since TP Morris opened his door to me at a time when so many others were closing theirs.

Alas, the *Limerick Weekly Echo and District Advertiser* is no more, the lean-to where we laboured over our modest news paragraphs, our opinionated match reports and our cures for catarrh is gone.

As I write (in the late spring of 1992) the *Irish Press* and its sister papers are preparing finally to leave Burgh Quay for a modern high-tech building in Parnell Square.

The ghosts of sixty years will be left behind and with them, it is hoped, the ill will that has dogged labour relations in the company for so long.

For Eamon de Valera's "great enterprise" it will be a new beginning—one that will lay the foundations for the next sixty years.

Michael O'Toole
1992

INDEX